MISSION CONTROL, THIS IS
APOLLO

The Story of the First Voyages to the Moon

MISSION CONTROL, THIS IS

APOLLO

The Story of the First Voyages to the Moon

ANDREW CHAIKIN WITH VICTORIA KOHL
★ ALAN BEAN ★

VIKING

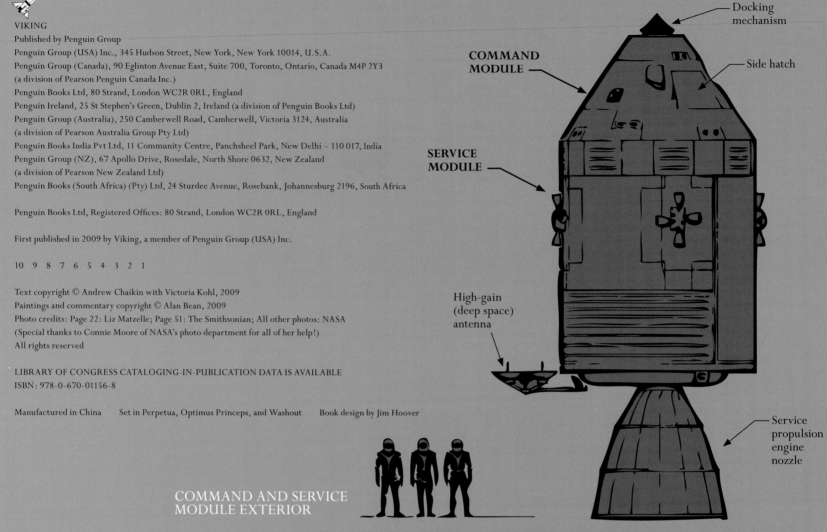

VIKING

Published by Penguin Group

Penguin Group (USA) Inc., 345 Hudson Street, New York, New York 10014, U.S.A.

Penguin Group (Canada), 90 Eglinton Avenue East, Suite 700, Toronto, Ontario, Canada M4P 2Y3
(a division of Pearson Penguin Canada Inc.)

Penguin Books Ltd, 80 Strand, London WC2R 0RL, England

Penguin Ireland, 25 St Stephen's Green, Dublin 2, Ireland (a division of Penguin Books Ltd)

Penguin Group (Australia), 250 Camberwell Road, Camberwell, Victoria 3124, Australia
(a division of Pearson Australia Group Pty Ltd)

Penguin Books India Pvt Ltd, 11 Community Centre, Panchsheel Park, New Delhi – 110 017, India

Penguin Group (NZ), 67 Apollo Drive, Rosedale, North Shore 0632, New Zealand
(a division of Pearson New Zealand Ltd)

Penguin Books (South Africa) (Pty) Ltd, 24 Sturdee Avenue, Rosebank, Johannesburg 2196, South Africa

Penguin Books Ltd, Registered Offices: 80 Strand, London WC2R 0RL, England

First published in 2009 by Viking, a member of Penguin Group (USA) Inc.

10 9 8 7 6 5 4 3 2 1

Text copyright © Andrew Chaikin with Victoria Kohl, 2009
Paintings and commentary copyright © Alan Bean, 2009
Photo credits: Page 22: Liz Matzelle; Page 51: The Smithsonian; All other photos: NASA
(Special thanks to Connie Moore of NASA's photo department for all of her help!)
All rights reserved

LIBRARY OF CONGRESS CATALOGING-IN-PUBLICATION DATA IS AVAILABLE
ISBN: 978-0-670-01156-8

Manufactured in China   Set in Perpetua, Optimus Princeps, and Washout   Book design by Jim Hoover

Docking mechanism

COMMAND MODULE

Side hatch

SERVICE MODULE

High-gain (deep space) antenna

Service propulsion engine nozzle

COMMAND AND SERVICE
MODULE EXTERIOR

This book is dedicated to our mothers, Nancy Chaikin and Sally Kohl,
who made sure when we were growing up that we had good books to read.
—ANDREW CHAIKIN AND VICTORIA KOHL

I dedicate this special book to my mother,
Frances Murphy Bean. She was as tough
and as dedicated as any army or marine
drill sergeant to changing me from a typical carefree boy into a worthy young man.
I did not know of the deep love and strong
character she must have possessed to guide
and encourage me day after day until I had
children of my own. It is because of her
that my paintings are in this book for you
to enjoy.
—ALAN BEAN

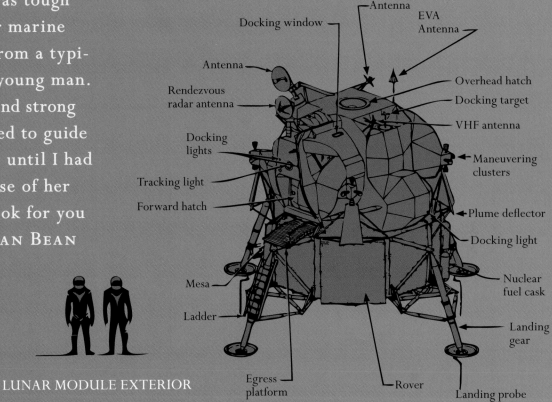

LUNAR MODULE EXTERIOR

- Docking window
- Antenna
- EVA Antenna
- Antenna
- Overhead hatch
- Rendezvous radar antenna
- Docking target
- VHF antenna
- Docking lights
- Maneuvering clusters
- Tracking light
- Plume deflector
- Forward hatch
- Docking light
- Mesa
- Nuclear fuel cask
- Ladder
- Landing gear
- Egress platform
- Rover
- Landing probe

★ CONTENTS ★

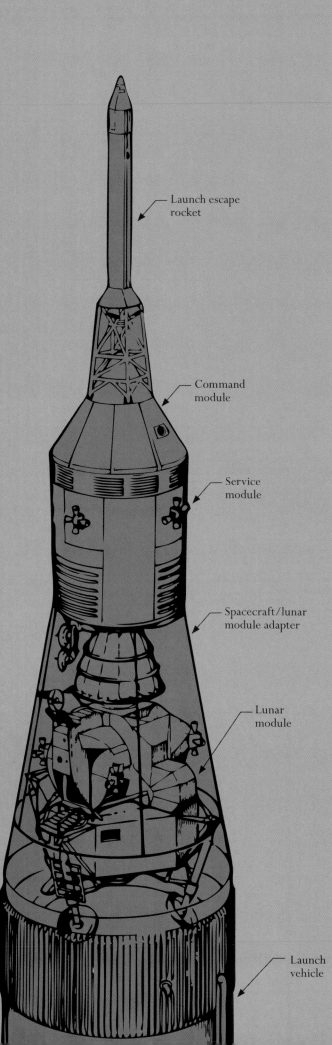

Launch escape rocket

Command module

Service module

Spacecraft/lunar module adapter

Lunar module

Launch vehicle

APOLLO SPACECRAFT LAUNCH CONFIGURATION
ATOP SATURN V ROCKET (FROM APOLLO 9 ONWARDS)

The launch of Apollo 10 and its Saturn V rocket, May 18, 1969.

THE SITES OF THE
APOLLO MOON LANDINGS

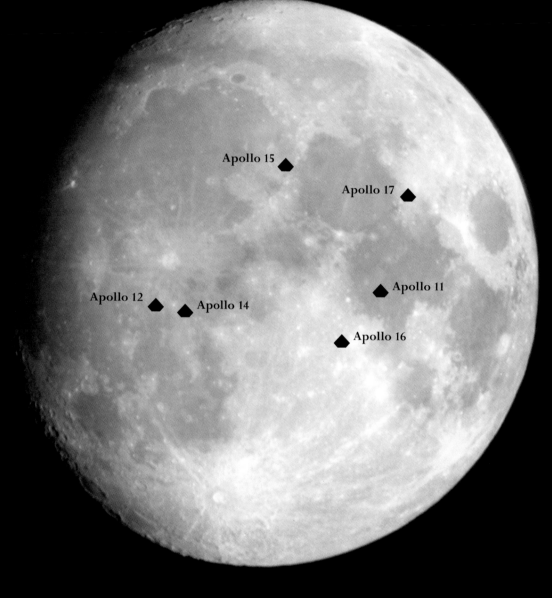

Apollo 15

Apollo 17

Apollo 12   Apollo 14

Apollo 11

Apollo 16

APOLLO 11
July 20, 1969: Sea of Tranquility

APOLLO 12
November 19, 1969: Ocean of Storms

APOLLO 14
February 5, 1971: Fra Mauro

APOLLO 15
July 30, 1971: Hadley Rille

APOLLO 16
April 21, 1972: Descartes Highlands

APOLLO 17
December 11, 1972: Taurus-Littrow Valley

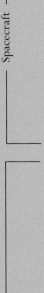

Spacecraft

Launch vehicle

Command module

Service module

Lunar module

Third stage

Second stage

First stage

APOLLO 101: A QUICK REVIEW

Here is an Apollo "cheat sheet," defining the spacecraft
and rockets, as well as frequently used terms.

SPACECRAFT

Command module (CM): The portion of the Apollo spacecraft that carried three astronauts to and from the moon. Since only the CM had a heat shield able to withstand the reentry into our atmosphere, it was the only portion to return to Earth. Together with the attached service module, it was called the **command–service module (CSM)**.

Service module (SM): Attached to the base of the CM, this provided electrical power, oxygen, and other supplies during the mission. It also contained the rocket engine used to get into and out of lunar orbit. The SM was discarded shortly before reentry.

Lunar module (LM, pronounced "lem"): The spacecraft used to land on the moon. It consisted of two separate pieces: The **descent stage** was used for the trip from lunar orbit down to the surface; left on the moon, it served as a launch platform for the **ascent stage**, which contained the astronauts' cabin as well as the rocket engine used to propel them back into lunar orbit.

Launch vehicle: A rocket used to launch a spacecraft. Many launch vehicles are composed of multiple **stages**, each of which has its own rocket engines. Since no one rocket can get the astronauts and their massive spacecraft into Earth orbit on its own, the stages work together to do the job. The launch vehicle used to send Apollo to the moon was called the **Saturn V**.

MANEUVERS IN SPACE

Transposition and docking: When the CSM separated from the third stage of the Saturn V, it turned around and linked up, or **docked**, with the LM, which had ridden into space on top of the third stage. After docking, the joined spacecraft separated from the third stage and continued its journey to the moon. Transposition and docking took place a bit more than three hours after launch. The CSM and the LM remained docked until it was time for the astronauts to land on the moon.

Undocking: About a day after entering lunar orbit, two astronauts entered the LM and separated, or **undocked**, from the CSM to begin their trip down to the moon's surface. The CSM, piloted by the remaining astronaut, orbited the moon for the duration of the lunar landing and exploration.

Rendezvous: The series of maneuvers one spacecraft makes in order to catch up with another spacecraft and match its orbit. During an Apollo landing mission, this happened when the two moonwalkers, after blasting off from the lunar surface in their LM's ascent stage, caught up with the third astronaut in the CSM. The two ships then re-docked, and when all three men were safely inside the CSM, the ascent stage was cast off for the CSM's return to Earth.

SATURN V ROCKET AND SPACECRAFT
ASTRONAUTS WERE FIRST CARRIED ON APOLLO 8; LM WAS CARRIED FROM APOLLO 9 ONWARD

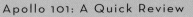

A WORD FROM THE ARTIST

I STARTED TAKING ART CLASSES when I was a test pilot in the early 1960s, well before I was an astronaut. None of the other pilots I knew did artistic things in their spare time, but I'd always liked to make things. When I was a boy, I'd put together countless model airplanes, and as an adult I built a lot of the furniture for our family. I wanted what I made to be functional and beautiful.

I enjoyed the art classes, but making art—the best art I could make at the time—was a struggle. (It is still that way today, even though the art seems much more advanced.) As my career as an astronaut progressed, I kept taking lessons and painted whenever I could.

In 1973, after I returned from my Skylab mission, a friend of mine asked me, "What are you going to do when you leave NASA and you quit being an astronaut?" I said I thought that wouldn't be for a while, but I might go to work for one of the major aircraft companies. She said, "I don't think you should. I think you ought to go be an artist." "Be an artist? That's crazy!" I replied. I hadn't even painted any space paintings.

But I couldn't get it out of my mind. I realized that I spent all of my spare time and energy on art; I didn't spend it thinking about working for an aircraft company!

So I took some time off from NASA and painted full-time to see if I'd like it. In space jargon, I "simulated" being an artist all day, every day. The more I simulated it, the more I realized that being a good artist was much more difficult than I'd thought. But at the same time, I liked it. I cared about it! I had many nice job offers for a lot of money, but I didn't care about them. I care about these paintings. I care about them every day.

I've been a full-time artist since I retired from NASA in 1981. Every painting I do has a story of its own, and the captions of the paintings in this book are shortened versions of those stories, in my own words.

—ALAN BEAN

Alan Bean's studio in Houston, Texas.

FRONT COVER *BIG AL AND HIS RICKSHAW (1983):*

Al Shepard is about to disassemble a double core tube. In front of him is his "rickshaw"—the Modularized Equipment Transporter (MET), the first wheeled vehicle on the moon. It was designed to carry tools and equipment to the work sites and return rock and soil samples to the lunar module. The MET was difficult to pull in the deep dust on the moon. It was difficult to draw and paint, too!

BACK COVER AND TITLE PAGE *TIPTOEING ON THE OCEAN OF STORMS (1982):*

An astronaut learns very quickly to run in a space suit. It's stiff at the knee and hip joints, but moves more easily at the ankle joints, so you use mostly ankle motion. It feels and looks as if you are dancing on tiptoe. I can remember running along next to this crater. Because of the moon's one-sixth gravity, I felt as if I could run forever and my legs would not get tired.

HALF TITLE *CONQUISTADORS (1986):*

As I worked on this painting of Apollo 15 astronauts Jim Irwin and Dave Scott, I was continually reminded how much astronauts on the moon resembled sixteenth-century conquistadors. Like them, we came in ships. Theirs were of wood, powered by wind and sail; ours were of advanced metals and plastics, moved by rocket engines. We each used the best technology of our age. But here the similarity ends. Conquistadors came to claim lands and gold and precious gems for their king or queen; we came for knowledge and understanding. We carried no weapons, just tools for digging and measuring. We were space-age conquistadors, and we truly came in peace for all mankind.

COPYRIGHT/DEDICATION *MOUNTAINS OF THE MOON—WITH THE LUNAR MODULE FALCON (1993):* Falcon, the Apollo 15 lunar module, sits on uneven ground, all alone on the plains of Hadley. The Apennine Mountains are about three miles behind it. We are near the eastern edge of Mare Imbrium, the dark circular sea that forms the right eye of the man in the moon when we view it from Earth. Claude Monet is my favorite artist; with him in mind, I have not painted the moon the neutral gray I saw with my astronaut-geologist's eye but rather the more beautiful combination of hues that I saw with my astronaut-artist's eye.

OVERLEAF *SCOUTING FOR THE RIGHT SPOT (1994):*

Pete Conrad has run ahead of me to find a place to deploy the experiments we would leave on the moon. We knew it wouldn't be an easy task for Pete, because there were craters as far as we could see in every direction. Pete finally spotted a perfect area about 600 feet from where we'd landed and set up our home on the moon. In the painting, I am carrying the experiments. It took us about two hours to unpack, set up, and align them. When the equipment was activated, the first thing it recorded was our own footfalls as we loped back to the lunar module.

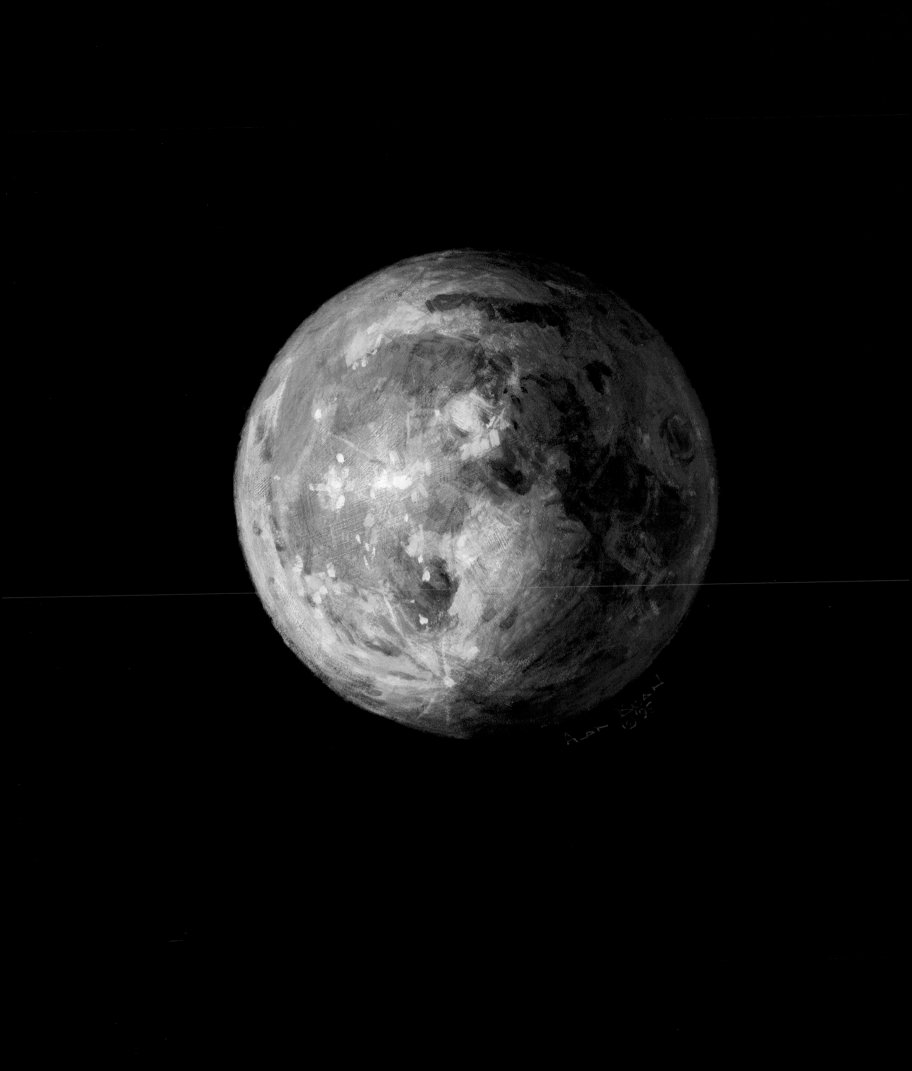

A MAN ON THE MOON

UNTIL 1961, SPACE travel was something that only dreamers and science fiction writers thought about seriously. But there were people who believed it was possible—not in some distant century, but in their lifetimes. Some of them became the engineers, scientists, and managers of the National Aeronautics and Space Administration, NASA.

This agency of the federal government had been created in 1958 to run the nation's space program. Back then, space was the new battleground of the cold war, the ongoing, tension-filled competition between the United States and the communist U.S.S.R. (Union of Soviet Socialist Republics) that began after World War II.

The Soviet Union had launched the world's first artificial satellite, *Sputnik 1*, into Earth orbit in October 1957. Americans were used to being first in everything, but now, in space, they were running second. And there was a chilling message in that small, beeping satellite: Big rockets like the one that launched *Sputnik* could also send nuclear weapons hurtling toward the United States at any moment. Everyone knew that having the best rocket technology wasn't just about exploration, but about *survival*.

When the United States finally launched its own satellite, *Explorer 1*, in January 1958, the space race really began. But by then the Soviets already had the first animal in space, a dog named Laika, and would soon have the first spacecraft to strike the moon and the first photographs of the lunar far side, which never faces the Earth.

In early 1961 NASA was eager to pull ahead by

A MOST BEAUTIFUL MOON (1995): I've painted a number of studies over the years to record some of my memories of seeing the moon close up. Here, I wanted to paint the moon in some of my favorite hues—not so scientific or realistic, but suggestive of the one created over 4.6 billion years ago. I hope my painting is just as beautiful and interesting to look at in its own special way.

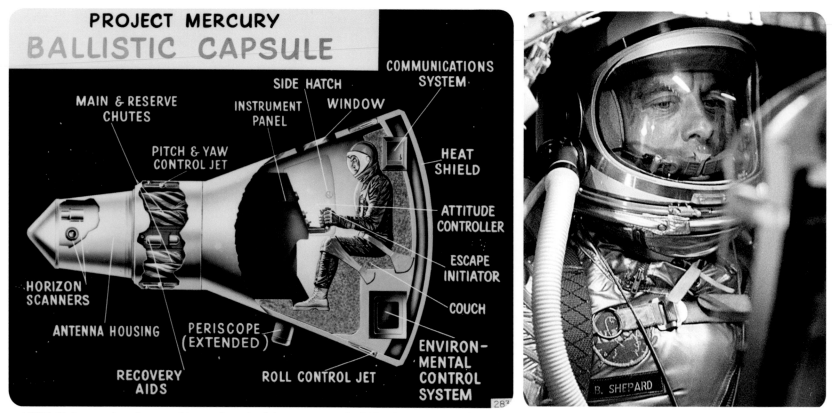

PROJECT MERCURY
BALLISTIC CAPSULE

COMMUNICATIONS SYSTEM
SIDE HATCH
WINDOW
MAIN & RESERVE CHUTES
INSTRUMENT PANEL
PITCH & YAW CONTROL JET
HEAT SHIELD
ATTITUDE CONTROLLER
ESCAPE INITIATOR
HORIZON SCANNERS
COUCH
ANTENNA HOUSING
PERISCOPE (EXTENDED)
RECOVERY AIDS
ROLL CONTROL JET
ENVIRON-MENTAL CONTROL SYSTEM
B. SHEPARD

LEFT: Cutaway drawing used to explain the Mercury capsule. RIGHT: Astronaut Alan B. Shepard Jr., the first American in space.

sending the first man into space with Project Mercury. But once again, the Soviets beat them to it.

On April 12, a twenty-seven-year-old Soviet pilot named Yuri Gagarin climbed into a spacecraft called *Vostok* (Russian for "east") atop a 100-foot-tall rocket and rode it into space. He landed 108 minutes later, after circling the Earth once. He was called a "cosmonaut," or cosmic voyager. With Gagarin's flight, Americans once again felt the sting of being second best.

No one felt it more than the new U.S. president, John F. Kennedy. He believed America *had* to win in space, to show developing countries looking for a powerful ally that America's free society was stronger and better than the communists'. The mighty rockets and complex spacecraft needed to win the space race would show that the United States also had the technology to defend itself and its allies. Kennedy felt sure the United States could catch up with the Soviets and even take the lead.

Only a few weeks later, NASA would put an American into space, in the first piloted flight of Project Mercury—but what should be the next step? After Gagarin's flight, Kennedy had an urgent question for Vice President Lyndon Johnson, who was overseeing America's space effort: "Do we have a chance of beating the Soviets by putting a laboratory in space, or by a trip around the moon, or by a rocket to land on the moon, or by a rocket to go to the moon and back with a man? Is there any other space program which promises dramatic results in which we could win?"

On May 5, 1961, Alan Shepard made a fifteen-minute suborbital flight in his Mercury capsule, *Freedom 7,* propelled by a Redstone rocket to a height of 116 miles and then splashing down in the Atlantic. Even though this wasn't as dramatic as Gagarin's flight, America had finally put a man in space, and the public's wildly joyous reaction reassured Kennedy that they would support the ambitious new space effort. But *how* ambitious? What he had in mind was off the charts.

On May 25, standing before a joint session of Congress, the president gave the United States one of history's boldest challenges: "I believe that this nation should commit itself to achieving the goal, before this decade is out, of landing a man on the moon and returning him safely to the Earth. No single space project in this period will be more impressive to mankind, or more important for the long-range exploration of space. And none will be so difficult or expensive to accomplish."

At NASA, the people who would have to make Kennedy's lunar visions real were stunned, inspired, excited . . . and nervous. There was an enormous gap between one fifteen-minute suborbital spaceflight and the dusty lunar surface 240,000 miles away, and they had to cross it in less than *nine years.* A new space race—to the moon—had begun.

BY THE SPRING of 1963, Project Mercury had put five more Americans in space; four of them had circled the Earth. NASA had learned how to send astronauts into orbit and bring them home safely. Today, that may sound pretty unremarkable. But until Mercury no one at NASA was certain a human being could survive a trip into space. The Soviets had said Yuri Gagarin and the other cosmonauts did just fine—but were they telling the truth? No one was sure. Unlike the U.S. space program, which was covered by TV, radio, and newspapers as it happened, the U.S.S.R.'s missions were conducted in secrecy. The rest of the world heard only what the Soviet government wanted it to know.

The last Mercury mission, flown by Gordon Cooper in May 1963, lasted more than a day. By then, the Soviets were putting cosmonauts in orbit for several days at a time. And in June, they launched the first

Launch of Friendship 7, the first U. S. manned orbital space flight. With astronaut John Glenn aboard, the Mercury-Atlas rocket rises from Pad 14.

woman into space, Valentina Tereshkova. It looked as if the United States was still losing the space race— but NASA was just getting warmed up.

Project Apollo, the effort to put Americans on the moon, was already being developed. Planners had a basic scheme for going to the moon, involving not one but two spacecraft, and they knew it would require complex, difficult things that Mercury hadn't even touched—things *no one* had ever done in space.

★ Astronauts would have to survive voyages lasting a week or more, long enough for a round-trip to the moon.

★ They would have to learn to work in the vacuum of space in order to take a moonwalk—what NASA called "extravehicular activity" (EVA).

★ After blasting off the moon's surface the astronauts in the lunar lander would have to chase down the mother ship, which would

Astronaut Edward White during the first American spacewalk, Gemini 4, June 3, 1965.

take them home, in a space rendezvous. In this complicated and *very* precise series of maneuvers, one ship was like a relay runner catching up with a second runner, while both raced around the track—at hypersonic speed!

★ Returning to Earth at 25,000 miles per hour, they would need to control their path through the atmosphere during their spacecraft's fiery reentry.

Before anyone could go to the moon, ways to accomplish these things would have to be developed and tested. Planners realized soon that NASA needed a bridge between the relatively simple Mercury flights and the awesome challenges of Apollo.

That bridge became Project Gemini. These two-man missions would be the training ground for the moon. And if NASA succeeded with Gemini, they would be on target to meet John Kennedy's challenge.

But the young president would not live to see it happen.

After Kennedy was assassinated in November 1963, Apollo and its end-of-the-decade deadline took on new significance, as a kind of memorial to the slain leader. Ironically, just two months before his death, Kennedy had proposed in a speech at the United Nations that the United States and the U.S.S.R. go to the moon *together*. He had asked, "Why . . . should man's first flight to the moon be a matter of national competition?" We will never know what might have happened had Kennedy lived.

THE SOVIETS WERE still winning the moon race. In the fall of 1964 they'd sent three cosmonauts into space in the first multiperson mission. Then, in March, less than a week before the first manned Gemini launch, they scored another triumph when Alexei Leonov became the first human to walk in space.

But each new Gemini mission brought NASA closer. Gemini 4's Ed White took a twenty-minute space walk. On Gemini 5, Gordon Cooper and Pete Conrad stayed in orbit for eight days, a world record. And then came the mission that put the United States in the lead for real.

In the fall of 1965, after the rocket for Gemini 6 failed to ignite, canceling the launch for astronauts Wally Schirra and Tom Stafford, NASA managers came up with a bold plan: the astronauts, on a mission now designated Gemini 6-A, would fly *during* the flight of Gemini 7, and try to rendezvous with them. In December, Gemini 7's Frank Borman and Jim Lovell were launched on a fourteen-day mission, and while in space were joined by Schirra and Stafford, who steered Gemini 6-A to within one foot of Gemini 7. It was the world's first space rendezvous.

But everyone knew that without warning, the Soviets might come up with another space first. The race to the moon was far from over.

When Project Gemini ended in November 1966 after two unmanned and ten piloted missions, NASA was on a high. There *had* been some serious problems. On Gemini 8, after the world's first space docking, Neil Armstrong and Dave Scott were almost killed when a malfunction caused their spacecraft to spin at the dizzying rate of once per second before Armstrong managed to regain control. And most of the spacewalking astronauts got so exhausted from working in rigid, pressurized space suits that their EVAs had to be cut short. But those problems were solved on later flights, and overall, Gemini was a spectacular

A view of Gemini 7, photographed from inside Gemini 6-A during the first U.S. space rendezvous, December 17, 1965.

Gemini 12 spacecraft photographed by Buzz Aldrin during one of his three EVAs, November 1966.

success, accomplishing all major objectives and bringing every astronaut home safely.

NOW NASA WAS ready for Apollo.

The sheer *scale* of the program was staggering. All around the country, thousands of people at NASA centers and aerospace contractors were hard at work creating the spacecraft for the lunar missions, the most complex flying machines ever devised.

There was a cone-shaped craft called the command

The F-1 engines of the Saturn V's first stage dwarf the moon rocket's creator, Wernher Von Braun.

service modules (CSM). The first Apollo missions would use only the CSM; on later flights, astronauts would test the lunar module (LM, pronounced "lem")—the world's first true spaceship—that they would use to land on the moon. And these amazing machines were only part of the story.

There were teams writing the intricate software for the CM's and LM's onboard computers. Others were developing the space suits and backpacks that moonwalking astronauts would wear. One group of scientists was choosing the best landing sites, using photos from NASA's robotic probes. Another was developing scientific experiments the astronauts would leave behind on the lunar surface. There were so many people all over America working on so many things that no one person could keep track of it all. Most of them never met one another—the man in Delaware who invented the zipper for the Apollo spacesuit didn't know the woman in Houston working on freeze-dried space food—but they were connected just the same, by the spirit of this bold adventure.

If anything conveyed the enormity of Apollo, it was the rockets being developed, which had to be bigger and more powerful; the Apollo spacecraft was larger and heavier than those used for Mercury and Gemini. A rocket called the Saturn IB would be used to send the CSM into Earth orbit. Its big brother, the giant Saturn V, would be capable of sending the entire Apollo spacecraft all the way to the moon. *If it worked.* Both the Apollo spacecraft and the Saturn V rocket were still untried, and it was all so complex, with so many things that could go wrong, that it would be a miracle if there *weren't* problems.

Still, as 1967 began, the engineers, managers, and astronauts of NASA were confident. With Gemini's successes behind them, they felt like a winning baseball team heading to the World Series. They were ready to reach for the moon.

module (CM); inside it, three astronauts would fly to and from the moon. They wouldn't have a lot of room to move around—about as much as a six-foot cube—but it was definitely better than Mercury and Gemini. In flight, the CM would be attached atop a cylindrical section called the service module (SM), which contained most of the astronauts' oxygen supply, fuel cells to provide electricity, and the large rocket engine they would use to get into and out of lunar orbit. Together, they were called the command-

The original seven Mercury astronauts from left to right: Carpenter, Cooper, Glenn, Grissom, Schirra, Shepard, Slayton.

HOW DO YOU choose people to go to the moon? That was what NASA had to figure out as it began selecting new astronauts for Gemini and Apollo. They would have to be comfortable with danger. They'd need quick reactions to handle emergencies, and high intelligence, to learn the complex systems and techniques of spaceflight. They would have to be in superb physical condition, to withstand launch and reentry, and prolonged weightlessness. NASA found these people among the ranks of military test pilots.

Test pilots are often the first to fly new kinds of planes, to see how they perform under all kinds of conditions. Their job requires them to handle—and even simulate—emergencies. They must fly very precisely to gather the data that engineers need to improve the aircraft's design. Many test pilots are trained engineers themselves, and can help with the design process.

All the Mercury astronauts had been test pilots, and so were the nine chosen for Gemini and Apollo in 1962. The new astronauts had advanced degrees in aeronautics or a new field called astronautics, which focused on how to build and fly space vehicles. And pilots with experience flying high-performance jets.

The following year NASA chose fourteen more astronauts, and this time, they included some pilots who had training in astronomy, physics, and even nuclear engineering, in order to help scientists develop new experiments for space missions. One, Buzz Aldrin, had a doctorate from MIT, where he did his thesis on space rendezvous.

In 1965, NASA recruited five professional scientists including a geologist named Jack Schmitt. Schmitt had never piloted an airplane, but he and the other scientists trained to fly the T-38 jets that astronauts used to commute between the space centers in Florida and Houston and the aerospace contractors around the country. Like the others, Schmitt had to work to become a good overall astronaut before he could be considered for a space mission.

Then, in 1966, nineteen more pilot-astronauts brought the total number to fifty-four, more than enough for the moon program. Some would act as support astronauts and some would wait many years for their chance to fly in space. And some would never fly at all, having been killed in jet crashes or disqualified because of medical

MERCURY MISSIONS

MERCURY-REDSTONE 3 (FREEDOM 7)
MAY 5, 1961
ALAN B. SHEPARD JR.
Duration: 15 minutes, 28 seconds
Achievement: First U.S. manned spaceflight;
first manned suborbital flight

MERCURY-REDSTONE 4 (LIBERTY BELL 7)
JULY 21, 1961
VIRGIL I. "GUS" GRISSOM
Duration: 15 minutes, 37 seconds
Achievement: Second manned suborbital flight

MERCURY-ATLAS 6 (FRIENDSHIP 7)
FEBRUARY 20, 1961
JOHN H. GLENN JR.
Duration: 4 hours, 55 minutes, 23 seconds
Achievement: First U.S. manned orbital flight

MERCURY-ATLAS 7 (AURORA 7)
MAY 24, 1962
M. SCOTT CARPENTER
Duration: 4 hours, 56 minutes, 5 seconds
Achievement: Second manned orbital flight

MERCURY-ATLAS 9 (SIGMA 7)
OCTOBER 3, 1962
WALTER M. SCHIRRA JR.
Duration: 9 hours, 13 minutes, 11 seconds
Achievement: Schirra made six orbits,
twice as many as Glenn or Carpenter

ATLAS 9 (FAITH 7)
MAY 15-16, 1963
L. GORDON COOPER JR.
Duration: 1 day, 10 hours, 19 minutes, 49 seconds
Achievement: First U.S. day-long orbital mission

*Pre-launch test of Mercury-Atlas 9 for the final Mercury mission,
Faith 7, May 1963.*

GEMINI MISSIONS

GEMINI 3
MARCH 23, 1965
VIRGIL I. "GUS" GRISSOM and JOHN W. YOUNG
Duration: 4 hours, 52 minutes, 31 seconds
Achievement: First manned Gemini mission.
Grissom and Young were the first astronauts
to change their spacecraft's orbit.

GEMINI 4
JUNE 3-7, 1965
JAMES A. MCDIVITT and EDWARD H. WHITE II
Duration: 4 days, 1 hour, 56 minutes, 12 seconds
Achievement: First multi-day U.S. spaceflight;
first U.S. spacewalk

GEMINI 5
AUGUST 21-29, 1965
L. GORDON COOPER JR.
and CHARLES "PETE" CONRAD JR.
Duration: 7 days, 22 hours, 55 minutes, 14 seconds
Achievement: First long-duration spaceflight

GEMINI 7
DECEMBER 4-18, 1965
FRANK BORMAN and JAMES A. LOVELL JR.
Duration: 13 days, 18 hours, 35 minutes, 1 second
Achievement: World record for long-duration spaceflight

GEMINI 6-A
DECEMBER 15-16, 1965
WALTER M. SCHIRRA JR. and THOMAS P. STAFFORD
Duration: 1 day, 1 hour, 51 minutes, 24 seconds
Achievement: First orbital rendezvous, with
Gemini 7

GEMINI 8
MARCH 16, 1966
NEIL A. ARMSTRONG and DAVID R. SCOTT
Duration: 10 hours, 41 minutes, 26 seconds
Achievement: First space docking (rest of mission
canceled due to spacecraft malfunction)

GEMINI 9-A
JUNE 3-6, 1966
THOMAS P. STAFFORD and EUGENE A. CERNAN
Duration: 3 days, 21 hours
Achievement: In-orbit rendezvous
(docking cancelled); spacewalk

GEMINI 10
JULY 18-21, 1966
JOHN W. YOUNG and MICHAEL COLLINS
Duration: 2 days, 22 hours, 46 minutes, 39 seconds
Achievement: First double rendezvous; two spacewalks

GEMINI 11
SEPTEMBER 12-15, 1966
CHARLES "PETE" CONRAD JR. and
RICHARD F. GORDON JR.
Duration: 2 days, 23 hours, 17 minutes, 8 seconds
Achievement: First single-orbit rendezvous; highest
Earth orbit ever reached; two spacewalks; first computer-
controlled re-entry

GEMINI 12
NOVEMBER 11-15, 1966
JAMES A. LOVELL JR. and
EDWIN E. "BUZZ" ALDRIN JR.
Duration: 3 days, 22 hours, 34 minutes, 31 seconds
Achievement: Rendezvous and docking; three
successful spacewalks; automatic re-entry

LEFT: Mercury Program patch   RIGHT: Gemini Program patch.

APOLLO ONE

JANUARY 27, 1967

COMMANDER: Virgil I. "Gus" Grissom
SENIOR PILOT: Edward H. White II
PILOT: Roger B. Chaffee
OBJECTIVE: First manned Apollo flight

"HOW ARE WE going to get to the moon if we can't talk between two buildings?"

You could hear the frustration in Gus Grissom's voice. On the afternoon of January 27, 1967, three weeks before their scheduled launch on the first manned Apollo flight, the veteran astronaut and his crew, Gemini 4 spacewalker Ed White and rookie Roger Chaffee, were sealed inside their command module high atop a Saturn IB booster on Pad 34 at Florida's Kennedy Space Center. Wearing space suits and helmets, they had entered the CM a few hours earlier for a practice countdown, in which the spacecraft would operate under its own electrical power. It was just like every other practice countdown for

all of NASA's previous piloted missions; it wasn't even considered dangerous.

Almost from the start, things didn't go right. First, there was a foul odor in the oxygen flowing through the astronauts' suits, which took an hour to fix. But finally, technicians sealed the crew inside the CM, closing its heavy, three-piece hatch and pressurizing its cabin with 100 percent pure oxygen.

Then came the communication problems. That was nothing new; the astronauts and ground teams had had trouble during almost every test. But today, as technicians inside two control buildings—one a few hundred yards away, the other five and a half miles

REMEMBRANCES OF A MOONWALK: SELF-PORTRAIT WITH FLAG (1984): This painting is part of a series relating to some of my feelings while I was on the moon. As you can imagine, I have many varied and vivid impressions and remembrances from the thirty-one hours spent on the Ocean of Storms with Pete Conrad, while Dick Gordon orbited sixty-nine miles above us in the command module. The mission at times seemed unreal and perhaps a little like a dream. Careful, considered actions gave way to instinctive reactions honed by years of intensive training. Words and logic can't explain these paintings completely, since they represent my feelings.

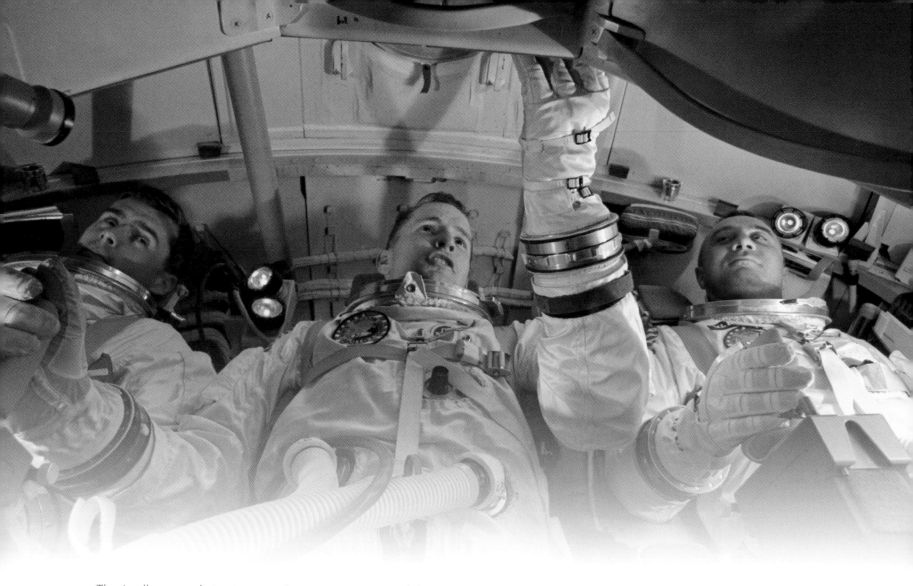

The Apollo 1 crew during training, January 19, 1967. From left to right: Chaffee, White, Grissom.

away—struggled to talk to the crew, Grissom could not hide his exasperation.

Like all the astronauts, Grissom knew it was normal to have problems with any new spacecraft, especially one as complex as the command module. No one had ever tried to build a moonship before, and Apollo 1 had so many parts and pieces that problems were inevitable. Everyone felt sure they'd be able to fix things in time for later missions. The goal right now was to get Grissom and his crew into space.

As night fell, giant floodlights came on, illuminating the 223-foot-high rocket and its launch tower. Technicians were still trying to fix the communications problems at about six thirty p.m. when suddenly, everyone heard chilling words over the

radio: *"There's a fire in the cockpit!"* Just twenty seconds after that, shock turned to horror as they heard a cry of pain—*"We're burning up!"*—and then, nothing.

At the launchpad, frantic technicians fought to open the hatch, but were driven back as the raging fire exploded through the command module's hull. They struggled, braving the intense heat, and after several desperate minutes finally got it open. But it was too late: Grissom, White, and Chaffee were dead.

SOMETHING HAD GONE horribly wrong—but *what?* Engineers took the burned wreckage of Apollo 1 apart piece by piece, examining even the tiniest screw. They re-created the fire inside a backup command module, and took movies of how the fire started, and how it spread. After a two-month investigation, they realized that a combination of things had caused the tragedy.

The insulation protecting some of the wires inside the CM had been worn away by workers climbing in and out. During the test, there must have been a spark from a frayed wire, and something nearby caught fire. Oxygen feeds a fire, and in the high-pressure, 100 percent oxygen atmosphere inside, the fire quickly became an inferno. Items in the cabin that would normally not have burned easily—for instance, strips of Velcro on the walls that the astronauts used to keep things from floating away in weightlessness—exploded as if they had been soaked in gasoline.

Once the fire started, the astronauts were doomed.

In the middle seat, Ed White had struggled to open the command module's 90-pound inner hatch by undoing a set of bolts. But the heat of the fire caused increased pressure that sealed it shut with thousands of pounds of force. And just twenty seconds after the fire began, it burned through the oxygen hoses for the astronauts' space suits, letting in smoke and toxic gases. The men soon fell unconscious and within min-utes, they were dead. No one could have saved them.

For everyone involved, the shock of the *Apollo 1* tragedy would never completely go away. Everyone knew spaceflight was dangerous, but no one had expected astronauts to die on the ground, during a routine test. Even more painful was the realization that it could have been prevented. For some, it was too much to bear; one manager had a nervous breakdown.

But there was only one thing to do: Fix the problems and move on. From now on, NASA would never pressurize a spacecraft with pure oxygen while it was on the launchpad. It would make sure everything inside the cabin was fireproof. It would protect the insulated wiring from damage. And it would replace the heavy, three-piece hatch with a single-piece hatch that could be opened in seconds. It would take many months of hard work to redesign the command module, both at NASA and at North American Aviation in California, where it had been designed and built. But there was still time to meet John Kennedy's challenge to carry out a lunar landing before decade's end.

Interior and exterior views of the Apollo 1 spacecraft after the fire.

APOLLO SEVEN

OCTOBER 11-22, 1968

(10 DAYS, 20 HOURS, 9 MINUTES, 3 SECONDS)

COMMANDER: Walter M. Schirra Jr.
COMMAND MODULE PILOT: Donn F. Eisele
LUNAR MODULE PILOT: R. Walter Cunningham
OBJECTIVE: First piloted flight of the Apollo command-service modules

IN THE FALL *of 1968, the awful memory of the Apollo 1 fire was still painfully sharp at NASA, but grim determination had given way to cautious excitement. There had been five unpiloted missions since the tragedy, including Apollo 4, the first test flight of the giant Saturn V moon rocket, and Apollo 5, the first unpiloted test of the Apollo lunar module (LM). Mostly, those missions had gone very well. Each brought NASA a little closer to the moon. But underneath the excitement there was relentless pressure.*

There was still heated competition with the Soviets. The Russians had suffered their own space tragedy a few months after the Apollo 1 fire, when cosmonaut Vladimir Komarov was killed during the first test flight of the new Soyuz spacecraft. But now there were signs that before the end of the year Soviet cosmonauts—not American astronauts—would make history's first flight around the moon. And in addition, everyone knew America had little more than a year to meet John Kennedy's lunar landing deadline.

Apollo 7 was the first piloted mission of the program, an eleven-day Earth-orbit test of the redesigned CM, which included all the improvements made after the fire. Assuming Apollo 7 was successful, NASA wanted the Apollo 8 Earth orbital mission to include the first piloted LM test flight. But the LM's development was way behind schedule, which led one of the managers in Houston to suggest an incredibly daring and dangerous idea: Send Apollo 8 around the moon instead, without a lunar module.

The plan had always been to carry a LM on every mission that went to the moon, even those that wouldn't try to land. If the service module's engine stopped working, astronauts could use the LM descent engine as a backup. Sending Apollo 8 to the moon without a LM made the mission riskier. But if NASA could pull it off, they would, in one step, dazzle the world, leap far past the Russians, and gain crucial experience in the techniques of flying to the moon and back, including navigation, precise rocket

Liftoff of Apollo 7 from Cape Kennedy Launch Complex 34, October 11, 1968.

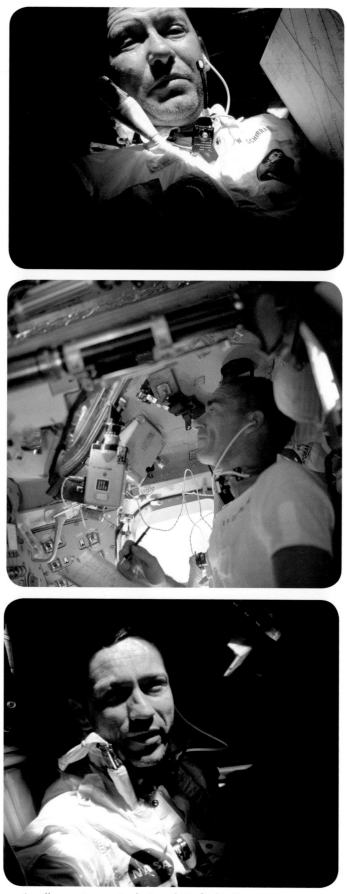

Apollo 7 astronauts during their flight. From top to bottom: Schirra, Cunningham, Eisele.

firings, communicating at lunar distance, and high-speed reentry.

Before they could do that, they would have to fly Apollo 7. If—and only if—everything went well on Apollo 7, the astronauts of Apollo 8 just might be spending Christmas orbiting the moon.

FLAME POURED FROM the base of the Saturn 1B booster, and its thunder echoed across the marshlands of the Kennedy Space Center on the morning of October 11, 1968. Rising slowly at first, then quickly gaining speed, it soared into the blue and, within minutes, was only a bright dot in the Florida sky.

Inside the Apollo 7 command module, Mercury and Gemini veteran Wally Schirra and rookies Donn Eisele and Walt Cunningham felt the thrill of heading for space, and throughout NASA everyone had a momentary break from the constant pressure of the last twenty months.

In January 1967, tragedy had struck Pad 34, and now, at this same launchpad, Apollo had finally found its wings. But no one could *really* relax. Not yet. If something went seriously wrong—if the mission failed or, much worse, if the three astronauts didn't make it back to Earth—would the Apollo program survive? No one knew the answer.

With each day of the mission and each new test aboard Apollo 7, the stress and uncertainty that had hung over NASA since the fire slowly lifted. No one had expected the redesigned command module to sail through its maiden voyage without any major problems. And yet—*it did!* Every system aboard Apollo 7, from the power-producing fuel cells to the onboard computer to the service module's big rocket engine, was working nearly perfectly. So perfectly, in fact, that beginning on the fourth day of the flight, mission controllers could relax and . . . watch TV.

The fuzzy black-and-white pictures on the big

★ WHEN YOU GOTTA GO, YOU GOTTA GO ★

IF YOU THINK everything about flying an Apollo mission was fun, think again. There was one part of living in space that the astronauts hated: going to the bathroom.

It wasn't just because they had to do it with two other guys in the room. The really nasty problem was weightlessness. Everything floats. *Everything.* So, what to do? When Apollo was being designed, there was no such thing as a space toilet. (The first one on a U.S. spacecraft was aboard the Skylab space station in 1973.) Apollo astronauts had to use the same system that had been developed for Gemini flights: hoses and bags.

For urination, there was a hose with a receptacle on one end. The hose was attached to a valve on the side of the command module cabin, and using that valve, the urine could be dumped into space. It worked well enough, although sometimes the hose could pop off while the astronaut was using it, letting droplets of urine float around in the cabin. (It was always a good idea to have paper towels handy.) When the valve opened and the urine was released into space, it quickly froze into ice droplets that sparkled in the sunlight. In fact, one astronaut, when asked "What was the most beautiful thing you saw in space?" answered, "Urine dump at sunset."

For "number 2," the facilities were even worse. There was a plastic bag whose opening had a strip of adhesive that the astronaut used to attach the bag to his rear end. After he was finished, he had to close up the bag, and worst of all, knead it to mix the feces with a germicide chemical to prevent the growth of bacteria. Then he would place the bag in a storage cabinet so that doctors could analyze it after the flight. The whole thing, from start to finish,

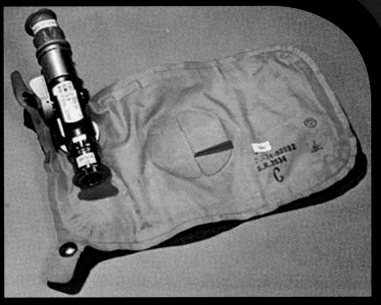

The urine transfer system.

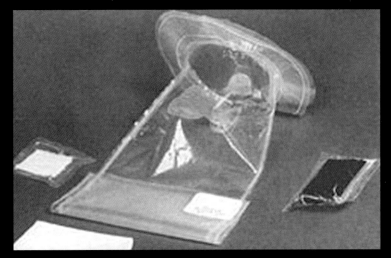

A fecal containment bag.

usually took forty-five minutes to an hour. And that was another reason astronauts tried to postpone pooping for as long as possible: They had to have an hour without more important work to do. To keep the need for defecating during the mission down to a minimum, the astronauts ate special diets designed to produce as little solid waste as possible, beginning about a week before launch.

LEFT: A playful moment during one of Apollo 7's Emmy Award-winning broadcasts. RIGHT: The Florida Peninsula viewed from Apollo 7.

screen in Mission Control were coming from a small TV camera aboard the spacecraft. For the few minutes that Apollo 7's signals were picked up by U.S. tracking stations, Schirra and his crew could share glimpses of their life in orbit, circling the planet at 17,500 miles per hour, 140 miles up. The picture wasn't anywhere near as good as regular TV, but it was coming from space, and it gave the astronauts a chance to show how much fun it was to float around inside the command module. Schirra held up specially made cards before the TV camera, often inspired by old-time radio shows. One read HELLO FROM THE LOVELY APOLLO ROOM, HIGH ATOP EVERYTHING; another, KEEP THOSE CARDS AND LETTERS COMING IN FOLKS. Down on earth, everyone was amazed; the pictures were better than anyone expected.

But that was true for just about everything during Apollo 7. Not only were all the systems humming along beautifully, but the astronauts accomplished all the tests and scientific experiments in their flight plan, and even took on a few extra ones added by Mission Control. Apollo 7 was turning out to be almost a picture-perfect mission. *Almost.*

Twenty-four hours after reaching space, Wally Schirra came down with a monster head cold, and Donn Eisele caught it, too. A cold is bad enough on Earth, but in the weightlessness of orbital flight, it's completely miserable. Nothing falls, so sinuses can't drain, and a stuffy head just stays stuffed. The grouchy Schirra lost his cool, and even argued with Mission Control—something that did *not* go over well at NASA.

Even this couldn't ruin everyone's satisfaction at knowing that the redesigned command-service modules had passed their first test with flying colors. For NASA, the recovery from the fire was finally complete. It was time to send Apollo 8 to the moon.

NIGHT LAUNCH (1975): This is the first space-related painting I ever attempted. I was inspired by the only night launch in the Apollo program, Apollo 17. I was so impressed with how beautiful it was, how the bright orange of the rocket exhaust stood out vividly against the night sky. I painted a number of studies, but I wasn't yet skilled enough to paint what I saw realistically, so I created this semi-abstract painting instead. Being an artist is a very demanding profession. Work and time and dedication are all needed in abundance.

APOLLO EIGHT

DECEMBER 21-27, 1968

(6 DAYS, 3 HOURS, 42 SECONDS)

COMMANDER: Frank Borman
COMMAND MODULE PILOT: James A. Lovell Jr.
LUNAR MODULE PILOT: William A. Anders
OBJECTIVE: First piloted flight to the moon

THE RADIO INSIDE Apollo 8 suddenly filled with static. Somewhere out there in the blackness was the moon, and now it was between the spacecraft and the Earth, blocking all contact with Mission Control. In the command module, Bill Anders knew they were on their own.

For almost sixty-six hours, he and his crewmates, Frank Borman and Jim Lovell, had coasted through the sunlit blackness of space. And now, in the early morning hours of December 24, 1968—Christmas Eve—they were about to go into orbit around the moon.

Anders looked out the side window of the Apollo 8 command module, into the darkness. To his surprise, during the trip out, he had not seen the moon at all; it was lost in the glare of the sun. But as the spacecraft drew nearer, they flew into the moon's shadow, and suddenly the sky was full of stars—except for a huge, round area where there were no stars at all, just blackness. Suddenly Anders realized that this "hole" in the stars was the darkened moon—and they were being pulled toward it. The hair stood up on the back of his neck. He quickly fought off the feeling and put his mind back on the job.

The "job" on Apollo 8 was one that no human being had ever had before. Almost everything about this

HOMEWARD BOUND (1994): On Christmas morning, 1968, the Apollo 8 crew had been circling the moon for twenty hours. But now it was time to fire—or "burn"—the service module engine and kick the spacecraft out of lunar orbit to begin the 58-hour voyage home. As an astronaut myself, watching from Earth, I was all too aware that this was only the second flight of a brand-new kind of spacecraft, and that its systems had to perform perfectly. There was no backup for the main rocket engine. If it did not work right, my friends might remain in lunar orbit forever. I painted the Apollo 8 spaceship as it emerged from behind the moon this last time, after the successful burn.

★ ALL THIS AND TURKEY, TOO ★

IF YOU'VE EVER eaten freeze-dried food, you've dined like an Apollo astronaut.

Since the space program began, one of NASA's biggest concerns has been minimizing weight. The reason is simple: the less weight you carry into space, the less fuel you need to get there. And with food, one of the easiest ways to reduce weight is to remove the water. This can be done by freezing the food, which turns the water to ice, and then putting the frozen food into a vacuum chamber. The vacuum causes the ice to evaporate, leaving behind a dried food that is only a fraction of its original weight and size (which also makes it easier to store). The freeze-dried food is then sealed inside plastic bags, which can be cut open when it's time to eat. In space, the astronaut adds water to the food before eating it. (The water supply comes from the service module's fuel cells, which combine hydrogen and oxygen to produce electricity, with water as a by-product.)

The astronauts had quite a variety of foods to choose from. Some were bite-size pieces, meant to be eaten dry. These included strawberry cereal cubes, bacon squares, beef sandwiches, and cheese-cracker cubes. The foods that could be rehydrated by adding water included spaghetti and meat sauce, chicken and vegetables, potato soup, and shrimp cocktail. There were also powdered beverages: orange drink, grapefruit drink, coffee, and cocoa. In the command module, the astronauts had hot water, which meant they could have hot meals. Because the lunar module had no hot water supply, astronauts on the moon had to make do with cold food and drinks.

Before the flight, each astronaut tried all the foods and picked out the ones he liked, and these were packed aboard the spacecraft. The menus for each day of the mission were designed by NASA's nutritionists.

At first, the space "cuisine" didn't get rave reviews. The food didn't have to be great, of course; it just had to keep the astronauts alive and healthy. Since no Apollo mission lasted longer than twelve days, the astronauts could put up with mediocre meals. But there were some bright spots.

On Apollo 8, a new type of meal called a "wet pack," developed for the military, was tried for the first time. Wet-pack meals weren't freeze dried; they were normal food that had been heat-sterilized to prevent spoiling, then sealed in metal pouches. Although wet-pack meals were heavier than freeze-dried ones, they also tasted better—and NASA was willing to include some in the astronauts' menu. On Christmas Day, as Frank Borman and his crew headed home from the moon, they enjoyed a wet-pack meal of turkey and gravy that had been put aboard as a surprise. By the later Apollo missions, there were more improvements, and for southern-born astronaut Charlie Duke, there was even a bit of home cooking on Apollo 16: freeze-dried grits.

Examples of Apollo meals and a water gun.

BREAKFAST

Canadian bacon

Applesauce

Strawberry cereal cubes

Cocoa

Toasted bread cubes

Orange drink

LUNCH

Pea soup

Chicken and gravy

Cheese sandwiches

Bacon squares

Grapefruit drink

DINNER

Shrimp cocktail

Beef hash

Cinnamon toasted bread cubes

Date fruitcake

Orange-grapefruit drink

LEFT: The Apollo 8 crew's menu for the day they spent orbiting the moon. RIGHT: Lovell, Anders, and Borman beside a simulator at the Kennedy Space Center, November 1968.

mission was a first. Borman, Lovell, and Anders were the first space travelers to actually *go somewhere*. They were the first people to ride the giant Saturn V moon rocket, the first to leave Earth orbit, and the first to see their home planet shrink to the size of a golf ball held at arm's length. (A planned flight around the moon by Soviet cosmonauts in late 1968 had never taken place.) Anders knew there was no guarantee they'd get back, either. After they fired the service module's rocket engine to go into lunar orbit, it would have to fire again, and work perfectly—there was no backup engine—to send them home, or they would be stranded with no hope of rescue.

His crewmates had flown in space before, but Anders was a rookie, and before the flight he'd thought about the risks he was taking. Everyone had worked as hard as possible for their safety, but Anders knew something might still go seriously wrong. Was it worth the chance that he might not come back, leaving his wife and five young children alone without him? Yes, he decided, it was, because Apollo 8 was important to the space program, and to the country. And also, it was his chance to be something he had wanted to be since childhood: an explorer. He was about to become one of the first humans to see the far side of the moon with his own eyes.

NOW THE THREE men were strapped into their seats, and at exactly the right moment they fired a four-minute blast of their service module's rocket engine. Then the engine shut down, and they were in lunar orbit. They had all seen the images sent back by NASA's robotic orbiters, but no picture could possibly have prepared the astronauts for what they now saw just sixty-nine miles below them.

Through the command module's windows, the men looked down on the side of the moon that is never seen from Earth. It was a scene of utter desolation: No air, no water, no life—just a barren expanse of craters and mountains. It reminded Anders of a deserted beach after a volleyball game, covered with footprints. To Borman, it looked more like a battlefield pounded by countless bombs. Lovell was struck by the complete lack of color in the surface: This was a black-and-white world. And because the moon had died, geologically speaking, billions of years ago, its landscape was also unimaginably ancient, almost as old as the solar system itself. It could not have been more different from the world they had left behind.

But Anders and his crewmates were not thinking about the Earth. For the next twenty hours, as they circled the moon ten times, they would be focused on this alien world. Jim Lovell would use the onboard navigation system to take sightings on lunar landmarks, giving mission planners important information about Apollo 8's orbit. Frank Borman, mean-

while, would keep the spacecraft oriented and make sure his crew didn't get too tired to do their jobs. And Bill Anders would observe and photograph the parade of craters and mountains passing below for scientists back on Earth. This truly was a new world to explore, and soon Anders was hard at work trying to probe its mysteries.

EXPLORERS OFTEN FIND things they never imagined. Certainly, on the first flight to another world, everyone expected the astronauts to make discoveries. For Anders, however, the biggest surprise—and the greatest discovery—didn't come from looking at this desolate, pockmarked world below him.

During Apollo 8's fourth orbit around the moon, as the spacecraft drifted around from the far side, Anders had just paused in his lunar photography work when suddenly, the Earth popped into view, rising above the moon's bleached horizon into the blackness of space. It was wrapped in brilliant white clouds, which stood out vividly against the deep blue waters of the Pacific Ocean. He could see a patch of reddish land, part of the great deserts of Australia. He could hardly believe how beautiful it was. Anders aimed his camera and began snapping photographs of humanity's first Earthrise. One of them would become one of the most famous pictures of the twentieth century.

From almost a quarter-million miles away, the Earth was so tiny that Anders could have hidden it behind an outstretched thumb. And yet, it was so precious. It was a world to be cherished. To human beings, it was everything. He began to realize, *We came all this way to study the* moon, *and it's really the* Earth *that's the most interesting part of this flight.*

On that Earth, it was Christmas Eve, and for many in Mission Control, and countless others around the world following the flight on TV and radio, the magic of that day added to the wonder of this first

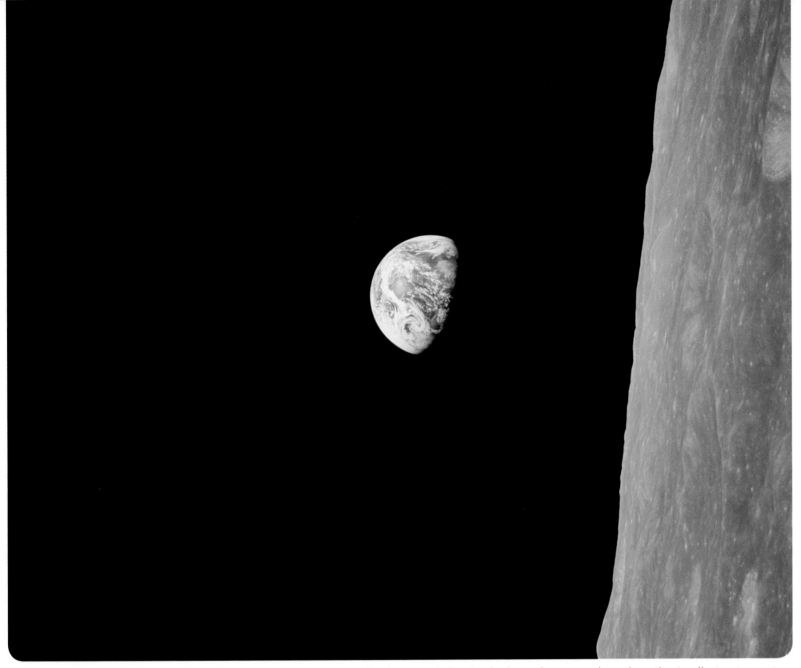

Earthrise, December 24, 1968. Although the photograph is usually shown with the Earth above the moon, this is how the Apollo 8 astronauts actually saw it as they came from behind the moon on their fourth orbit.

lunar voyage. Borman, Lovell, and Anders added a crowning touch when they broadcast a television show during their eighth lunar orbit that concluded with a surprise reading of the first ten verses of the biblical book of Genesis. As the TV show concluded, Borman said, "Good night, good luck, and God bless all of you—all of you on the good Earth."

A few hours later came the moment of truth. Strapped in their seats once more, flying over the far side of the moon, the men counted down the seconds until they would reignite the service module's rocket engine to speed them out of lunar orbit and onto a course for home. In Mission Control, everyone waited in tense silence to see whether the engine had worked. They wouldn't know until almost twelve minutes later, when Apollo 8 coasted around the far side and reestablished radio contact.

When the moment finally came, shortly after midnight on Christmas Day, the message that crackled across space from Jim Lovell could not have been more appropriate, or more welcome: "Please be informed, there is a Santa Claus!"

APOLLO NINE

MARCH 3-13, 1969

(10 DAYS, 1 HOUR, 54 SECONDS)

COMMANDER: James A. McDivitt
COMMAND MODULE PILOT: David R. Scott
LUNAR MODULE PILOT: Russell L. "Rusty" Schweickart
OBJECTIVE: First piloted flight of the Apollo lunar module

"OKAY, YOU'RE FREE!" From inside the Apollo 9 command module *Gumdrop*, Dave Scott called out across empty space to his crewmates Jim McDivitt and Rusty Schweickart, who were floating away inside one strange-looking flying machine. It looked less like a spacecraft than a giant mechanical insect, with four legs, two triangular windows for "eyes," and a gaping hatchway of a "mouth." The Apollo 9 lunar module certainly lived up to its name, *Spider*.

But there was a very good reason the LM looked so weird: it was the first true spaceship, designed to fly only in the vacuum of space. It didn't need to have smooth sides, like the CM, because it would never battle air resistance. It didn't matter that it had skinny metallic legs and rocket nozzles and antennae sticking out every which way. Or that in some places it didn't even have walls, just gold foil. It had one job, and that was absolutely crucial: On the upcoming lunar landing missions, it would carry two astronauts down to the surface of the moon, serve as their home while they explored, and then bring them back to their crewmate in lunar orbit. It didn't matter what the LM looked like. All that mattered was that it worked.

During Apollo 9's launch, the LM had rested within a set of protective panels at the top of the Saturn V's third stage. A few hours into the mission, Scott

THE SOURCE OF INTELLIGENT LIFE, DETAIL (2006): As I looked at our beautiful planet Earth from our small command module windows, I thought of all the humans who were out there living their lives on that little blue and white ball. It just did not seem possible that the tens of thousands of people I had seen at sporting events and on TV and at shopping malls and driving around in their cars—much less the 6.7 billion that are alive on our planet right now—could really all be held on that tiny sphere by gravity, so that they didn't fly off into space.

The crew of Apollo 9. Left to right: McDivitt, Scott, and Schweickart.

triggered a set of explosive bolts, and the CSM separated from the LM and the third stage. After pulling away, Scott pointed *Gumdrop*'s nose at the roof of the LM. Then he slowly closed in until the two ships met. A device called a docking probe on *Gumdrop*'s nose slid into a cone-shaped receptacle called a drogue on *Spider*'s roof, and a series of latches snapped shut to hold the two firmly together. Then Scott pulled the docked spacecraft away from the now-unneeded third stage. Later, Scott removed the probe and drogue from *Gumdrop*'s docking tunnel, so his crewmates could enter the LM.

As *Spider* did a slow turn so that Scott could inspect and photograph it, he could see the LM's two pieces. The bottom half, called the descent stage, contained the rocket engine for the moon landing, as well as four landing legs, and storage compartments for experiments to be placed on the lunar surface. The top half, called the ascent stage, had the crew cabin where McDivitt

and Schweickart now were, along with the controls and flight instruments. That tiny cabin would be bedroom, dining room, and office for future moonwalkers. It also had the windows, the radio, and clusters of small maneuvering rockets. And, most important, it had the engine that would blast the astronauts off the moon and back into lunar orbit.

The engineers at Grumman Aerospace who designed and built the LM had one of the toughest jobs in the entire Apollo program. They started in 1962 with nothing more than ideas, skill, and determination—and it took them seven years of incredibly hard work to turn these into the most exotic flying machine ever created. Everything in the LM had to be as lightweight as possible. And everything in it had to be specially created, often by hand.

There had been many problems with the LM—with the rocket engines, the environmental control system, the radar it would need to rendezvous with

ON THE SECOND day of the Apollo 9 mission, something happened to Rusty Schweickart that he had never expected. He was floating in the command module's lower equipment bay, a wide area at the foot of the seats, putting on his space suit. For a few seconds, he had no sense of up or down, and then, suddenly, he threw up. He managed to keep his mouth closed until he could find an air sickness bag. After that, he felt fine, and his crewmates didn't even tell Mission Control about the incident. But four hours later, Schweickart was in the lunar module throwing switches, when he vomited again. Once again, he felt much better soon afterward, but this time mission commander Jim McDivitt asked the doctors in Houston for advice.

The doctors were not surprised. They had known that weightlessness might cause problems for an astronaut's balance organs, located within the inner ear. In orbit around the Earth or the moon, or flying between the two worlds, an astronaut is in a state of freefall. And so the balance organs send signals to the brain that say, "I'm falling. I'm falling. I'm still falling." But the astronaut's eyes send a different message to the brain; they say, "I'm rightside up," or "I'm upside down," or "I'm sideways," depending on how the astronaut is turned within the spacecraft, and they also say, "I'm *not* falling." This "argument" between the eyes and the inner ear, which scientists call "sensory conflict," can make a person sick. Moving around inside the spacecraft often makes the problem worse.

This hadn't come up on Mercury and Gemini, because those spacecraft didn't have any room to move around; the astronauts were pretty much stuck in their seats. But the Apollo command module was roomier, and on Apollo 9 there was even a second spacecraft attached— the lunar module—at the end of a tunnel. Just as not

Rusty Schweickart adjusting his communications microphone.

a boat, not every astronaut would become spacesick. But Schweickart turned out to be one who did.

For a few days, his illness was a concern to doctors especially because he was planning to make a space walk later in the mission, to test the lunar space suit and backpack. If he threw up inside his helmet, the doctors worried, he might be in danger of choking on his vomit.

But after a couple of days, Schweickart seemed to be completely recovered, and he was able to make his space walk after all, with no problems.

Today, space motion sickness is part of what doctors call "space adaptation syndrome," a condition that affects about half of the astronauts who go into space. In most cases, it goes away on its own after a few days. Scientists believe this is because the brain learns to interpret the mixed signals from the eyes and inner ear—in other

the command module—and they had delayed this first piloted test flight for several months. That was one of the reasons NASA had decided to send Apollo 8 around the moon, without a LM, giving Frank Borman and his crew the chance to make history. But to the crew of Apollo 9, making the first Earth orbit test flight of the complete Apollo spacecraft—command ship and lander—was just as exciting.

As Dave Scott watched his friends pull away, he knew they were risking their lives: *Spider* had no heat shield, so it could not carry them back to Earth. For six hours, flying free, McDivitt and Schweickart would venture more than 100 miles from the safety of *Gumdrop*'s cabin. They had to find out if all the LM's problems had been solved, by testing each of *Spider*'s systems. There was always the chance that something could go seriously wrong. If that happened, if McDivitt

and Schweickart could not make it back to the command module, Scott would have to rescue them.

But they didn't need his help. Everything on *Spider* worked perfectly, from the rocket engines to the radar. Six hours later, Scott looked out the window and saw a tiny dot in the blackness. Slowly it grew larger, until he could see those triangular "eyes," and the gaping hatchway "mouth" of the LM's ascent stage. *Spider* was coming back to him—or at least half of it was. McDivitt and Schweickart had left the descent stage behind, circling the Earth, just as future moonwalkers would leave theirs on the surface of the moon when they headed back to their command module.

Someday, Scott knew, a command module pilot in lunar orbit would see this same strange sight. And he would feel just as happy as Scott did right now.

The lunar module Spider *as seen from* Gumdrop, *the command module.*

APOLLO TEN

MAY 18-26, 1969

(8 DAYS, 3 MINUTES, 23 SECONDS)

COMMANDER: Thomas P. Stafford
COMMAND MODULE PILOT: John W. Young
LUNAR MODULE PILOT: Eugene A. Cernan
OBJECTIVE: Dress rehearsal for the lunar landing

FLYING OVER THE far side of the moon, the descent engine of the lunar module *Snoopy* spewed its invisible flame into the vacuum of space. Thirty seconds later, right on schedule, it shut down again. Inside, Gene Cernan scanned the readout from the onboard computer, which told him that *Snoopy* was now in a new orbit, one that would take him and his commander, Tom Stafford, to an altitude of 50,000 feet—just nine miles above that barren, pockmarked surface, sixty miles closer than Apollo 8 had come. Through the LM's small, triangular windows, Cernan and Stafford saw the curve of the moon's horizon begin to flatten out. They were on their way down. Soon they would be closer to the moon than anyone had ever been.

Like all the astronauts, Stafford and Cernan would have loved to go *all* the way down and land on the moon, but that was not their mission. Everyone at NASA was amazed that Apollos 7, 8, and 9 had gone so well—

but the managers thought it was still too risky to try a landing until they knew more. The crew of Apollo 10 was assigned to test the complete Apollo spacecraft in lunar orbit. They would do everything required for a lunar landing mission—except the landing itself. Flying *Snoopy* down to its low point, Stafford and Cernan would scout the planned Apollo 11 landing site on the moon's Sea of Tranquility. Then, firing *Snoopy*'s engines once more, they would head back to their crewmate John Young in the command module *Charlie Brown* for the trip back to Earth. If—and *only* if—everything went right on Apollo 10, NASA would give the okay for Apollo 11 to try to land.

You might think that getting to within nine miles of the moon and *not* being able to land would be frustrating. But Cernan and his commander had known for almost a year that they would not be the ones to take that historic step. Landing on the moon was such

IF YOU COULD have been at the Kennedy Space Center on May 18, 1969, at 12:49 p.m. Eastern Standard Time, you would have seen, heard, and felt something incredible. At that moment, a giant Saturn V rocket lifted off from Pad 39A, splitting the air and shaking the ground with its tremendous roar, trailing an enormous column of fire, and propelling the crew of Apollo 10 toward the moon.

The very idea of even going to the moon would have been impossible without the Saturn V, the most powerful rocket ever created. (The Soviet Union built a rocket almost as big, but it blew up every time they tried to launch it, and that was one of the main reasons their manned moon program failed.)

Everything about the Saturn V was mind-boggling. When topped by the Apollo spacecraft, it stood 363 feet tall, making the whole thing 60 feet taller than the Statue of Liberty, or longer than a football field. The rocket's enormous size meant NASA had to create a special Vehicle Assembly Building—a giant cube more than 50 stories high—to put it together. At liftoff, the Saturn V weighed more than 6 *million* pounds. Most of that weight was the fuel and oxidizer burned by the rocket engines of the Saturn's three stages. The energy stored in those propellants was equivalent to the power of a small atomic bomb.

Five engines on the first stage produced a total of 7.5 million pounds of thrust—more than the combined power of 300 F-15 jet fighters! Burning kerosene and liquid oxygen, the first stage engines had enough fuel to fire for about two and a half minutes, long enough to send the astronauts to a height of about 40 miles. At that point, the first stage fell away and the second stage engines ignited, burning liquid hydrogen and liquid oxygen and producing a million pounds of thrust. During the next six minutes they boosted the craft almost high enough and fast enough to reach low Earth orbit. Finally, the second stage separated—like the first stage, it would land somewhere in the Atlantic—and the third stage's single hydrogen-oxygen engine, with 200,000 pounds of thrust, fired for almost three minutes to place Apollo in Earth orbit. Later, the engine was reignited to send the astronauts toward the moon.

It's still amazing to realize that during the Apollo program twelve of these enormous beasts were launched, and almost every one worked perfectly (and the few problems that did occur were later fixed). Or that there were only two unpiloted test flights of the Saturn before the Apollo 8 astronauts rode it to the moon. The last Saturn V, launched in 1973, placed the huge Skylab space station in Earth orbit. And then the great moon rockets—each of which could be used for only one flight—were abandoned. Instead NASA chose to develop the reusable Space Shuttle, which they hoped would lower the cost of getting into space.

Today, three Saturn Vs still exist; each had been built to launch moon missions that were later canceled. They are on display at the space centers in Texas, Florida, and Alabama, reminders of a time when Americans reached for the moon, and made it.

LEFT: The Apollo 10 Saturn V rocket in the Vehicle Assembly Building (VAB).
TOP RIGHT: Stafford, Cernan, and Young in front of "their" Saturn V.
BOTTOM RIGHT: The first stage being trucked to the VAB.

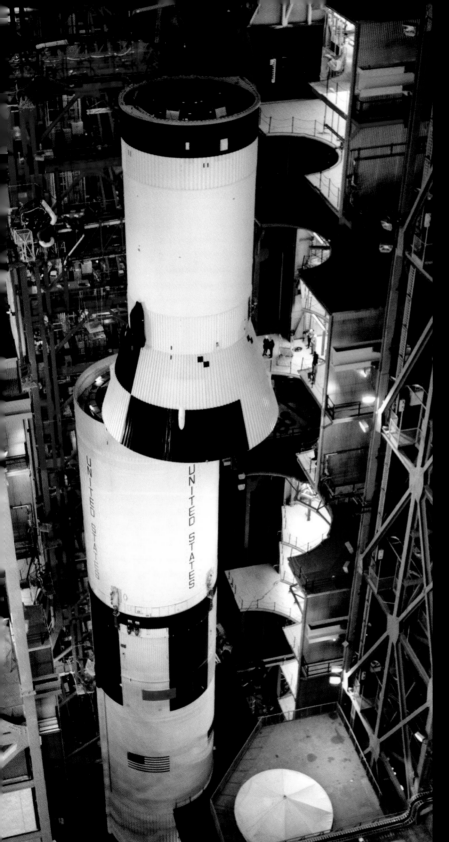

an enormous challenge, and there were still so many unanswered questions. NASA needed to see whether two different spacecraft in orbit around the moon could talk to each other, and to Mission Control 240,000 miles away. They needed to find out how the command ship and lander might be pulled off course by the moon's uneven gravity. Stafford, Young, and Cernan had come to the moon to get the answers.

Apollo 10 was part of the step-by-step approach that was the key to Apollo's success, with each new mission building on the accomplishments of the last. Of course, like most astronauts, Cernan dearly wanted to walk on the moon—and still hoped he might have that chance on some later mission. But he also felt lucky to be on *any* Apollo flight, especially one as important as Apollo 10.

As *Snoopy* coasted lower and lower, Cernan and Stafford had a view of the moon like no humans before

them. The mountains looked close enough to touch. Finally they were down to 50,000 feet, a height they had flown at many times on Earth, in jets—but never as fast as this. *Snoopy* was now moving at a speed of 3,700 miles per hour through the vacuum of space. In Mission Control, astronaut Charlie Duke, serving as capcom (short for "capsule communicator," the one person who talks directly to the astronauts) could hear Cernan's excitement: "Houston, this is *Snoopy*! We is Go and we is down among 'em, Charlie!"

Speeding over the Sea of Tranquility, Stafford and Cernan had a close view of the planned Apollo 11 landing site. It looked smooth near the center, Stafford told Houston, but if the LM came down near the edges, the astronauts might have to dodge large craters and boulders. If so, they'd better have enough fuel to maneuver around and look for a safer spot.

Hours later, he and Cernan were getting ready to

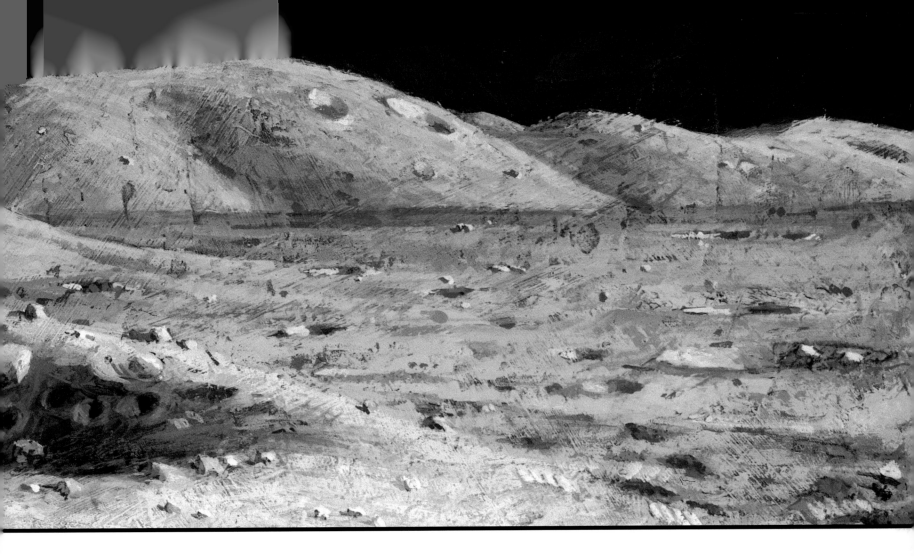

cut their descent stage loose before heading back to the command module. But before they could do that, *Snoopy* began to tumble out of control. Through his window, Cernan suddenly saw the moon's horizon spin wildly, and he let out a curse, not remembering that everyone in Mission Control could hear him. If they didn't do something—*fast*—they would never recover.

With a test pilot's lightning-quick instincts, Stafford punched the button to cast off the LM's heavy descent stage. Now he could fire the small rocket thrusters on the ascent stage and stop the spin. Finally, *Snoopy* calmed down and was flying normally again. But to everyone involved in Apollo, it was another reminder of the most important rule of space-flight: *Never forget that this is dangerous business, and things can go wrong at any moment.*

Soon, a burst from *Snoopy*'s ascent engine sent Stafford and Cernan on their way back to rejoin John Young in *Charlie Brown*. The following day, all three men headed back to Earth, proud of their part in the amazing string of successes that had finally cleared the way for the crew of Apollo 11—Neil Armstrong, Buzz Aldrin, and Mike Collins—to fly the boldest mission in history.

PORTRAIT OF A CRATER, FIRST EFFORT (1992): Apollo 10 astronaut Gene Cernan came within 69 miles of the lunar surface. Later, as part of Apollo 17, he would leave his footprints here, on Ballet Crater. We are in the Taurus-Littrow Valley of the moon. As an astronaut, I would have observed that the rocks and surface material were dense aphanitic basalts ranging from a light to a dark gray, but as an artist I created a painting that is a slightly warm green in the sunlit areas, with cool, colorful violet shadow. I feel that I am not an astronaut who paints but rather an artist who was once an astronaut.

APOLLO ELEVEN

JULY 16–24, 1969

(8 DAYS, 3 HOURS, 18 MINUTES, 35 SECONDS)

COMMANDER: Neil A. Armstrong
COMMAND MODULE PILOT: Michael Collins
LUNAR MODULE PILOT: Edwin E. "Buzz" Aldrin Jr.
OBJECTIVE: First lunar landing

BACK ON EARTH, before the flight, every-one—absolutely *everyone*—had asked Neil Armstrong the same question: What are you going to say when you step onto the moon? To their surprise, the man who would become the first person to walk on an-other world didn't have an answer. He really hadn't given it much thought.

He had more important things to worry about—like *how* to land on the moon. The lunar landing was the most difficult task anyone had ever attempted in space. And so, as he and Buzz Aldrin floated into their lunar module, *Eagle*, on July 20, 1969, orbiting the moon, Armstrong wasn't thinking about what he'd

say when he took that historic step. He was just hoping he'd have the chance to take it.

Even as he and Aldrin undocked from Mike Col-lins in the command module *Columbia* and prepared to descend to the surface, Armstrong wasn't at all sure they would succeed. And there wasn't much point in thinking up a quote he might never get to use.

MORE THAN ANYTHING else, Neil Armstrong loved to fly. Ever since he'd gotten his pilot's license at the age of sixteen, in 1946—before he learned to drive a car—he'd mastered all kinds of flying ma-chines. There was the fighter jet he flew during the

THE FIRST HUMAN FOOTPRINT (1995): This is a moment that will live in history books forever: July 20, 1969. I have painted Neil Armstrong lifting his left foot from the moon's dusty surface. He, and we, can see the first human footprint placed anywhere in our vast universe other than on our tiny planet Earth. There will be many other first footprints in our future—first footprint on Mars, first on an asteroid, first on a moon of Jupiter, and first on a planet around a star other than our sun—but none so future-changing as this one.

The Apollo 11 crew and their rocket. From left to right: Armstrong, Collins, and Aldrin.

Korean War in the early 1950s, taking off from the deck of an aircraft carrier—and, even more difficult, *landing* on it. And after the war, when he became a test pilot, there were greater challenges. Armstrong was one of the handful of men to fly the sleek black arrow called the X-15, a rocket-powered airplane that could go many times the speed of sound, soaring to the edge of space. He'd even flown in space before as commander of Gemini 8, making the world's first space docking, in 1966. That mission had almost cost

him and Dave Scott their lives, when their spacecraft began tumbling out of control. Armstrong's coolness in the face of danger had saved them.

But landing on the moon was like no other flying that Armstrong—or anyone else—had ever done. The main difference was that the moon has no atmosphere, making wings and parachutes useless. There was only one way to control your speed as you descended to the moon's surface, and that was to use the thrust of a rocket engine. Depending on how you pointed the

HARD DRIVING (1988): Buzz Aldrin is driving a core tube into the moon's surface in order to get a continuous sample of surface and subsurface soil. He is finding it more difficult then he anticipated—much harder than his training on Earth. A core tube is a hollow metal pipe with a sharp-edged bit on the leading edge. It is attached to a tool extension handle so that it can be driven into the surface from a standing position. Buzz managed to get a five- or six-inch core sample for the scientists back on Earth.

engine as it fired, you could change your horizontal speed or your vertical speed, or a combination of both. It got pretty complicated, and that was the reason the LM's computer would control the engine during most of the descent.

The computer could fly *Eagle* all the way to the ground if Armstrong let it, but he wasn't about to do that—because the computer had no way of knowing if they were about to come down in a crater or onto a field of boulders. During those final minutes of the descent, Armstrong would let the computer handle some of the flying; specifically, he would let it control the thrust of the engine. But *he* would steer the lunar module to a safe landing spot. (Despite Buzz Aldrin's designation as "lunar module pilot," his job included no flying. During the landing, Aldrin would monitor systems, operate the computer, and relay important data to Armstrong.)

That is, if everything worked.

For the last seven months Armstrong and Aldrin had spent countless hours doing practice landings inside the lunar module simulator at the Florida space center. It had a copy of the LM's cabin, with all the same instruments and controls, all run by computers. Outside, a team of instructors had thrown all kinds of problems at them to test their skill. And Armstrong had even flown a strange and dangerous flying machine called the LLTV (Lunar Landing Training Vehicle) that actually let him feel what it was like to fly a LM in the moon's one-sixth gravity. By the time Apollo 11 left Earth, Armstrong felt ready for the real thing. Still, he knew the actual landing would be the ultimate test, not just for him and Aldrin but for the teams of flight controllers in Mission Control.

IN A SENSE, there weren't just three people flying every Apollo mission; there were dozens. The astronauts were the ones who physically controlled the command module and lunar module. But they relied on teams of experts in Mission Control at the space center in Houston to look over their shoulders, and help them solve any problems that came up.

Many of these specialists were in their twenties, just a few years out of college. But they were sharp. And before each mission they went through countless simulations to practice every crucial event. During a flight, these controllers sat in a special room called the Mission Operations Control Room, or MOCR (pronounced MOH-ker). Each controller had a console with a TV screen that would show all kinds of information, especially data about the spacecraft's fuel supply, the electrical system, the engines, and so on. The computers onboard the spacecraft were limited, with less memory than a cell phone has now. But in the basement of Mission Control there were entire rooms full of computers, and sometimes, the controllers knew more about how the spacecraft was functioning than the astronauts did.

Sitting in the front row—the controllers called it "the trench"—were the specialists who kept track of the spacecraft's flight path and figured out the rocket firings that the astronauts needed to make to stay on course. The second row included the flight surgeon, who kept watch over the astronauts' health; a controller called EECOM, who monitored the crafts' electrical and environmental control systems; and the capcom (capsule communicator), an astronaut who was usually the only person in Mission Control to speak directly to the Apollo crew. And in the third row was the leader of all the mission controllers, the flight director, whose job description was one sentence long: *The flight director may take any action necessary for crew safety and mission success.*

Task Accomplished: The celebration in Mission Control after Apollo 11's splashdown, July 24, 1969.

On Apollo 11, there were three different flight directors, each with his own team of controllers, assigned to different eight-hour portions of the flight. For the lunar landing, the man in charge was thirty-five-year-old Gene Kranz, a veteran of Mission Control since the beginning. Like their colleagues, Kranz and his team went through countless hours of preparation for their role in the landing, including many practice runs with all manner of simulated problems. And when the real landing came, all that preparation turned out to be absolutely crucial—especially when the computer alarms sounded.

It was twenty-six-year-old Steve Bales, the controller in charge of monitoring the lunar module's computer, who had to analyze the situation. Like the other controllers, Bales had his own team of experts to help him. And fortunately, in one of the last simulations before the mission, they'd faced just this kind of problem. Seconds after Armstrong and Aldrin reported the alarms, Bales was able to tell Kranz that it was okay to continue. It wasn't the first time that a flight controller saved a mission, and it would not be the last.

Now *Eagle* began its descent to a bright, cratered moonscape, its engine firing. It would take about twelve minutes for the trip from 50,000 feet down to the surface. With only enough fuel for one try, there were three ways this could end: They would abort, they would crash, or they would land.

As Aldrin was reading off the numbers of diminishing altitude and speed, just as he had always done in the simulator, suddenly an alarm rang in the astronauts' headsets: there was a problem with the computer. It had too many things to do, and it was threatening to stop working. If that happened, it meant a certain abort.

Tense moments passed while they waited for an answer from Mission Control, and then it came: *Keep going.* They could work around the problem, and the computer would still do its job.

But now Armstrong had a new problem: when he looked out the window at the moon, a thousand feet below him, he saw that the computer was taking them straight into a giant crater. It was as big as a football stadium, with boulders all around it the size of small cars. Though the boulders would have been very interesting to explore, Armstrong realized it was too dangerous to try to land there. And so he flipped a switch and took over from the computer to guide *Eagle* to a safer spot. Cruising over the moon, he saw the cratered landscape come closer and closer. Now they were just 100 feet up—and finally he saw a good landing area.

FOR ONE PRICELESS MOMENT (1986): Here are Neil Armstrong and Buzz Aldrin completing, in my opinion, the most significant thing they did during their historic journey: raising the American flag. It was only a few minutes later that President Richard Nixon, calling by telephone from the Oval Office in the White House, said, "For one priceless moment in the whole history of man, all the people on this Earth are truly one; one in their pride in what you have done, and one in our prayers that you will return safely to Earth."

He flew *Eagle* lower, heading almost straight down and slowing its speed, keeping his eye on rocks and craters to avoid. But then, his view of the surface became confused by blurry streaks: It was *blowing dust*. They were so close that *Eagle*'s descent rocket was kicking up powdery soil from the moon's surface.

Closer and closer *Eagle* came, dust blowing furiously, as Armstrong struggled to see the lunar surface. He knew they were getting low on fuel. Now Mission Control sent a warning:

Only sixty seconds of fuel left before they would have to abort.

Now thirty seconds. But they were so close!

At last, the three spindly metal probes attached to *Eagle*'s footpads touched the surface, and a blue light on the instrument panel suddenly came on. "Contact light," called Aldrin, and the lunar module settled gently onto the ground. Armstrong shut down the engine and watched in amazement as the blowing dust sailed away in all directions and disappeared. Then everything was still. The men ran through a quick series of postlanding steps and enjoyed a moment of celebration, shaking hands and grinning at each other.

Then Armstrong sent a message to a waiting world: "Houston, Tranquility Base here. The *Eagle* has landed." From Mission Control, he heard capcom Charlie Duke answer, "You've got a bunch of guys about to turn blue. We're breathing again. Thanks a lot."

Now that they were on the moon, the first task was to prepare the LM's systems to leave, in case there was an emergency. But everything was work-

Neil Armstrong's first photo after setting foot on the moon.

ing beautifully, and soon they knew they were there to stay. Twenty hours later, after taking history's first moonwalk and getting some sleep, they would lift off to rejoin Collins in lunar orbit.

But right now, there was time to eat lunch. And there was time, too, for Armstrong to finally think about those words everyone back on Earth was waiting for.

As far as he was concerned, he and Aldrin had become the first men on the moon *together*, at the moment of touchdown. Armstrong felt sure that *walking* on the moon would be far easier than *landing* on it had been. But he knew how focused everyone was on the moon-

LOCKING UP THE ROCKS (1985): Neil Armstrong is locking up one of the two containers of lunar samples Apollo 11 brought back. The containers are specially designed to seal the rocks and soil in the moon's vacuum until they can be returned to Earth. All Apollo landings were made with the sun to the rear of the LM so that the craters and boulders would be most visible during the landing descent. After landing, the area in front of the LM is then in total shadow, and this is where Neil stands. To my delight, this effect worked beautifully, with Neil somewhat dark yet colorful in shadow and the Sea of Tranquility a bright counterpoint.

walk, and particularly on his first step. He would be the first one to climb down the ladder attached to *Eagle*'s front landing leg, until he was standing on a foil-covered footpad. The step from the footpad onto the surface would not be a big one, but it would surely be a hugely important one in human history. As he thought about that, Armstrong knew what he would say.

Seven hours after landing, after he and Aldrin had tended the LM's systems and eaten, they put on their special lunar backpacks, helmets, gloves, and boots. After releasing the oxygen from *Eagle*'s cabin they opened the front hatch, and Armstrong crawled out onto the platform at the top of the front landing leg. Carefully, he climbed down the nine rungs of the ladder and hopped down to stand on the footpad. Just as he had done many times in training, he radioed a description of what he saw for everyone on Earth.

And then, Neil Armstrong raised his left foot and placed it on the ancient dust of the moon. He tested his weight, and he spoke for the ages: "That's one small step for a man, one giant leap for mankind." After all the fuss, he hoped everyone felt it was worth the wait.

THE EAGLE *IS HEADED HOME (1983): The Apollo 11 lunar module,* Eagle, *is about to make history's first lunar liftoff. Neil Armstrong, at the left window, and Buzz Aldrin, at the right, are ascending from Tranquility Base to rendezvous with Mike Collins in the orbiting command module,* Columbia, *some 69 miles above them. After transferring themselves and their treasure of moon rocks to the command module, they will head for home. I remember my own liftoff from the moon as a big bang followed by what felt like a super-fast elevator ride. The big bang was the reverberation of the explosive bolts separating the ascent stage from the descent stage. The rest of the ride was quiet because, in the airless environment of the moon, the rocket makes no sound.*

APOLLO TWELVE

NOVEMBER 14-24, 1969

(10 DAYS, 4 HOURS, 36 MINUTES, 24 SECONDS)

COMMANDER: Charles "Pete" Conrad Jr.
COMMAND MODULE PILOT: Richard F. Gordon Jr.
LUNAR MODULE PILOT: Alan L. Bean
OBJECTIVE: First landing at a prechosen spot on the moon

ALAN BEAN CLIMBED down the ladder on the front leg of the lunar module *Intrepid* and took his first steps onto the surface of the moon. He knew there must be lots of people who expected him to have historic thoughts—*Pete and I are the third and fourth humans ever to walk on the moon!*—but in truth, his mind was on his job. First, he would take a few minutes to get used to walking in the moon's one-sixth gravity. And then, there was work to do—lots of it.

A few hours ago, Bean and his commander, Pete Conrad, had made history's second lunar landing, touching down on a vast plain called the Ocean of Storms. Now they were taking the first of two moonwalks, each lasting about four hours. On their wrists each of them wore a checklist of the tasks ahead. Today, they had to set up a collection of scientific experiments; they would also collect samples of lunar rocks and dust for the scientists back on Earth. Then they would climb back into *Intrepid* for a meal and a night's sleep. Tomorrow, they would take a second moonwalk to explore and collect more samples. And they would even pay a visit to a fellow lunar explorer, a robotic spacecraft called *Surveyor 3*, that had landed on the Ocean of Storms two and a half years earlier, on the slope of a wide, old crater.

Landing within walking distance of *Surveyor* had been one of Apollo 12's most important goals. On Apollo 11, Neil Armstrong and Buzz Aldrin had not

ASTRONAUTA OPTIMUS MAXIMUS (2006): If Pete Conrad turns slightly from where he stands, he can see our lunar module on the other side of Surveyor Crater. He knows our lives depend on it—it is the only way home and there is no backup. But Pete is as cool as they come. "Doesn't that LM look neat, sitting on the other side of that crater?" Register another Pete Conrad moment! How fortunate I was to be standing on an alien world with such a man—in my opinion, the best and greatest astronaut—and such a friend.

LEFT: Pete Conrad exiting the lunar module. RIGHT: Alan Bean descending Intrepid's ladder.

been sure exactly where they had landed on the moon's Sea of Tranquility; even Mike Collins, searching from the orbiting command module, couldn't spot them with his onboard sextant. But now that Conrad and Bean were right where they intended to be, just 600 feet from Surveyor 3, NASA had shown that astronauts could land at a pre-chosen place on the moon. That would be especially important for future missions, which would be sent to explore some of the moon's most intriguing features.

Bean understood all of this as he took his first lunar steps on November 19, 1969. He also understood how lucky he was to be here—and, especially, to go to the moon with Pete Conrad as his commander.

To Bean, Conrad was the best there was at being an astronaut. It wasn't just because of his talent as a pilot (he fit the old saying, "He could fly any airplane, or the crate it came in") or because he knew so much about spaceflight. It was his instinct for making the right moves at the right time. No matter

what kind of situation he was faced with, on Earth or in space, Pete Conrad knew how to handle it.

He had proved that during Apollo 12's launch, when the Saturn V flew through a thunderstorm and the spacecraft got struck by lightning, knocking out the command module's electrical system. Another astronaut might have aborted the flight—and no one would have blamed him if he did—but Conrad stayed cool. His experience, and his instincts, told him the Saturn V was okay. Later, after they reached Earth orbit, the astronauts were able to revive the electrical system and keep going. Conrad's coolness had helped save the mission.

Now that they were on the moon, Bean was amazed at how much fun his commander was having. You would never have known that he was almost a quarter of a million miles from home, surrounded by the deadly vacuum of space. He was laughing and humming and having such a good time that back on Earth, some of the reporters covering the flight

★ CLOTHES MAKE THE MOONWALKER ★

NOT LONG BEFORE Alan Bean climbed out of the lunar module *Intrepid* and set foot on the Ocean of Storms, he thought of some women he'd met in Dover, Delaware. They were the seamstresses working at the International Latex Corporation, putting together his space suit. And Bean thought to himself, *I hope those ladies cared as much about their work as I do right now.* He had a very good reason to feel that way: Once he left the safety of *Intrepid*'s cabin, that suit was the only thing saving him from certain death.

Because the moon has no atmosphere, standing on its surface is the same as standing in the vacuum of space. Human beings need oxygen to breathe, of course, and they also need pressure, to keep blood and other liquids inside their bodies from turning to gas and bubbling away. On Earth, at sea level, the air presses against us at 14.7 pounds per square inch. You can do just fine with quite a bit less than that, though, and the Apollo space suits were pressurized with pure oxygen at about 3.8 pounds per square inch—which was also the pressure needed to give the astronaut the same amount of oxygen he would have had on the Earth's surface. The astronaut wore his oxygen supply in a special backpack called the Portable Life Support System.

The engineers who designed the space suit had a tough challenge: it had to be strong enough to hold its pressure, but it also had to be flexible enough to allow the astronaut to move around on the moon. The answer turned out to be a combination of things. At the elbows and knees, the designers used bellows, made with pleats like those in a flexible soda straw. And to help the astronaut bend, they put a series of cables within the suit to help it move correctly. They used layers of special materials, including foil, to protect the astronaut from intense heat and cold, ultraviolet light from the sun, and tiny, fast-moving grains of rock and dust called "micrometeorites." And then there was the need to keep the astronaut cool.

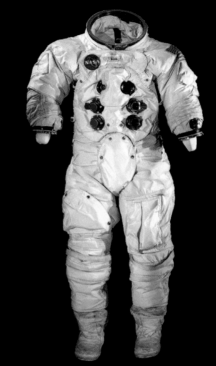

Alan Bean's suit, now at the National Air and Space Museum.

That was taken care of by a special pair of long underwear, which was covered by about 300 feet of narrow plastic tubes. Cold water from the backpack was pumped through the tubes, letting the astronaut stay cool no matter how hard he worked. The backpack also contained the radio for the moonwalkers to communicate with each other and with Mission Control. And it had an emergency oxygen supply, in case the primary system failed.

With all that gear, the space suit and backpack truly did serve as a portable spacecraft. And as the Apollo missions progressed, the suits improved. Beginning with Apollo 15, designers added a new bellows joint to let the moonwalkers bend at the waist so that they could ride in the lunar rover. And new zippers made the suits easier to take off and put on. That meant the astronauts could go to sleep in the LM's cabin without the discomfort of wearing the bulky suits. Of course, they still had to be careful to make sure the zippers and other moving parts didn't become clogged by moon dust. But to get a good night's sleep, it was worth the trouble.

wondered if he was on some kind of oxygen high. But Bean understood that this was just another aspect of Pete Conrad at his best: They'd get their work done, and they'd have a great time doing it.

SEVENTEEN HOURS LATER, as he emerged from *Intrepid* for the second time, Alan Bean was an experienced moonwalker. Yesterday, he and Conrad had accomplished all their work with few problems. Their scientific experiments were set up and working. Packed away inside *Intrepid* was a collection of lunar rock and dust samples. Now they would build on that success with their second moonwalk, including the visit to *Surveyor 3*. Bean was more than ready.

He'd discovered during yesterday's moonwalk how easy it was to work in lunar gravity, which is only one-sixth as strong as Earth's. Training on Earth wearing his space suit and backpack, Bean weighed about 360 pounds. Here on the moon, he weighed only 60 pounds. And everything he handled, from cameras to tools to rocks, weighed only one-sixth of what it would weigh on Earth.

Of course, there were some challenges. You had to have strong hands to grip tools like the rock hammer because you were always fighting the stiffness of the pressurized gloves. And then there was the business of running. Because the suits did not bend easily at the waist or the knee, Bean found it was best to let his legs stay straight and bend at the ankle. He would push off with one foot, then land and push off

CARRYING OUT ALSEP (2001): I can remember my building frustration as I carried the ALSEP—the Apollo Lunar Surface Experiments Package—to the deployment site. In the moon's one-sixth gravity, the two pallets (one with six experiments, the other with a nuclear generator) bounced up and down as they had not on Earth. The carry pole was flexing so much I was afraid it might break! I worked out a slow walk-then-stand-still technique, and finally got to the site, the experiments a little dusty but undamaged.

with the other, rocking from side to side as he ran. Running on the moon was an experience all its own, completely unlike running on Earth.

Now, as he and Conrad headed toward the crater where *Surveyor 3* sat, they had a chance to run for several minutes. Each time Bean's foot landed in the dust, a spray of particles shot out from where it hit, each dust grain following its own small arc, like a tiny cannonball. And *he* was like a cannonball, too. With each new step he launched himself into space, and it seemed to take a long time for him to come down. Amazingly, while he was "airborne," his calf muscles relaxed, so that during each step, he got a brief rest. It seemed he would never get tired.

And on this long run to the *Surveyor* crater, Bean had a chance to do something that wasn't on his checklist: absorb the awesome reality of where he was.

As he ran, Bean stole a moment to look up into the blackness high overhead, where he found a glowing blue-and-white crescent: Earth. Earlier he'd fought back his own sense of wonder at the place, keeping his mind on the job. But now he allowed himself a moment—just a moment—to let it sink in. He said to himself, "This is the moon. That is the Earth. I'm really here!"

ROCK 'N' ROLL ON THE OCEAN OF STORMS
(2002): Pete Conrad and I were on our second moonwalk when Houston asked us to check our suits and backpacks. As we rested, Pete saw a rock that he wanted, but it was too big for his tongs, and our space suits made it difficult to kneel down. As Pete looked at the rock, I looked at a strap on the bag attached to his backpack, and had an idea. I could hold the strap and lower Pete to get the rock. As I did, he called out, "Let me roll, a little bit over. . . . Atta boy!" That's how we demonstrated the first rock 'n' roll anywhere other than planet Earth. It was a special moment in lunar history, but was it a moment in music history? You can be the judge.

APOLLO THIRTEEN

APRIL 11–17, 1970

(5 DAYS, 22 HOURS, 54 MINUTES)

COMMANDER: James A. Lovell Jr.
COMMAND MODULE PILOT: John L. Swigert Jr.
LUNAR MODULE PILOT: Fred W. Haise Jr.
OBJECTIVE: First science-oriented lunar landing mission

USUALLY, THE LAUNCH of a new moon mission was a time of great excitement for everyone at NASA. But when Apollo 13 left Earth on April 11, 1970, it was a time of sadness for astronaut Ken Mattingly. For almost a year, he had been training to be Apollo 13's command module pilot. While mission commander Jim Lovell and lunar module pilot Fred Haise trained to explore the highlands near the lunar crater Fra Mauro in the first science-oriented mission to the moon's surface, Mattingly had prepared for his own solo explorations from lunar orbit. Meanwhile, their backup crew—John Young, Jack Swigert, and Charlie Duke—trained to carry out the same mission, in case, for some reason, Lovell and his crew could not make the flight. But no one expected that to happen. Everyone thought Lovell, Mattingly, and Haise would fly to the moon together, just as all of the other Apollo crews had.

Then came a shock. Less than a week before launch, NASA doctors learned that Charlie Duke had caught German measles from the child of a friend. Blood tests showed that Lovell and Haise were immune to the illness—but not Mattingly. And so, even though he was perfectly healthy, the doctors grounded Mattingly, refusing to let him fly. They feared he *might* get sick during the mission, and they just would not take that chance. In his place, his backup Jack Swigert joined Lovell and Haise and headed for the moon.

Two days later, on the evening of April 13, Mattingly was in the control center in Houston. Everything on the flight was going perfectly, but Mattingly hadn't been able to lift himself out of his own deep depression. Then, suddenly, with a single report from Apollo 13, everything changed. In Mission Control they heard Jim Lovell say, "Houston, we've had a problem."

Tense times in Mission Control. Astronauts pictured include Gene Cernan (in white shirt); to his left, seated, Edgar Mitchell, and Alan Shepard. Ronald Evans (later, Apollo 17 CMP) stands behind Mitchell.

That was an understatement.

While doing some routine chores aboard Apollo 13, Lovell, Swigert, and Haise heard a loud bang and felt the spacecraft shudder. When they looked at the instrument panel of their command module *Odyssey*, they saw signs of serious problems with the electrical system. There was also trouble with the onboard computer. And even worse, *Odyssey*'s oxygen supply was decreasing. When Lovell looked out the window, he saw some kind of gas streaming into space—and it didn't take long for him to realize that chilling sight explained the falling oxygen readings on his instruments.

What had happened? Probably an explosion, but what had caused it, no one knew. What *was* clear was that *Odyssey*'s three power-producing fuel cells, which used hydrogen and oxygen to generate electricity, were weakening; soon they would be dead. Everyone knew that, according to the mission rules, if even *one* fuel cell stopped working, the mission had to be aborted.

With sinking hearts, Lovell and Haise realized that they were not going to land on the moon after all. And then all three men began to understand that the situation was even more serious: with *Odyssey* starved

(OVERLEAF) APOLLO 13 . . . HOUSTON, WE HAVE A PROBLEM (1995): *The explosion of oxygen tank number two was the defining moment in the voyage of Apollo 13. This would begin some of America's finest hours in space flight. I have painted the explosion as a number of individually distinct particles streaming away from the tank. I do not believe an explosive cloud forms in the vacuum of space as it does on Earth, because everything I saw move in space traveled in a straight line. This painting was created to celebrate the motion picture* Apollo 13, *directed by Ron Howard and starring Tom Hanks, Bill Paxton, Kevin Bacon, and Gary Sinise.*

Original Apollo 13 crew. Left to right: Lovell, Mattingly, Haise.

EVEN BEFORE APOLLO 13 left Earth, NASA managers had to make a decision that would have a major effect on the flight. Should they pull Ken Mattingly off the crew and replace him with his backup, Jack Swigert? It wasn't a simple choice. If they left Mattingly on the crew, he might come down with German measles during the flight. If they postponed the mission for a month, to give enough time for Mattingly to recover (that is, *if* he got sick), they would add millions of dollars to the cost of the mission. And what if they replaced him with Swigert? In many ways, that was the best choice.

Like all the Apollo missions, Apollo 13 had two crews, a prime and a backup. Everyone assumed that the prime crew would be the ones to fly the mission, but just in case something went wrong, the backup crew went through the same training. That meant hour after hour in the simulators, practicing every phase of the mission, including how to respond to all kinds of possible emergencies. It meant study sessions and field trips with geologists who were training them to explore the moon. It meant learning every step in the complex flight plan. In short, the backup crew had to be just as ready to fly as the prime crew.

John Young, Jack Swigert, and Charlie Duke had trained hard as the backups for Jim Lovell's crew—up to a point. But by the time NASA was thinking about replacing Ken Mattingly, Swigert and his crewmates had already backed off, because it seemed certain they *wouldn't* fly Apollo 13.

Furthermore, the managers weren't talking about using the entire backup crew, just Swigert. And Jim Lovell was worried about that because of one thing: communication. During months of training, a space crew develops its own particular way of talking, especially during an intense mission phase such as the rendezvous between the command module and the lunar module, when they use a kind of verbal shorthand. Would Swigert be able to fit in with Lovell and Haise's style of communicating? There was only one way to find out. And so, just a couple of days before launch, Swigert was in the simulator with Lovell and Haise, testing the new team.

In the end, Lovell felt comfortable with the swap—although he was sorry to lose Ken Mattingly. As painful as the whole episode was for the astronauts, it showed that the Apollo training system worked: backup astronauts really can step in at the last minute, if necessary.

The final crew. Left to right: Haise, Swigert, Lovell.

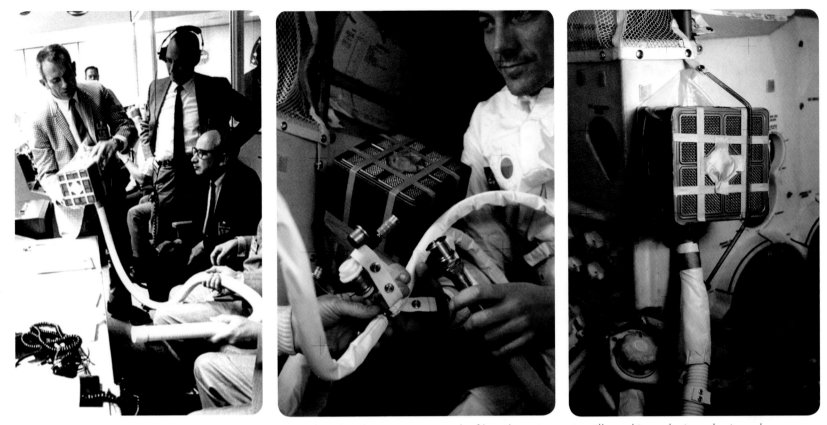

An improvised life saver. LEFT: In Mission Control, Deke Slayton examines the filter the astronauts will need to make in order to reduce carbon dioxide in the LM. CENTER: Swigert after the filter swap. RIGHT: The filter in place.

for power and losing its oxygen supply, the astronauts would be dead in a matter of hours. They had to do something—and *soon.*

In Mission Control, Mattingly—who had instantly snapped out of his own depression when the crisis struck—watched and listened as a stunned team of flight controllers struggled to solve the life-threatening problems aboard Apollo 13. At the time of the explosion, the astronauts were 200,000 miles from Earth, too far away to turn around and come back. The only workable plan was to continue on their course to the moon, fly around it, and head for a splashdown several days later. But with a dying command ship, how would the men last that long?

With just minutes of power left in the command module, there was only one answer—the lunar module *Aquarius,* attached to *Odyssey*'s nose. The LM had its own supplies of oxygen and electricity, its own computer, and its own rocket engines, but everything had

been turned off before launch, to save battery power. The men had just fifteen minutes to activate the lander, a job that normally took a couple of hours—and they did it, just in time. Swigert stayed behind in *Odyssey* long enough to shut down its systems, then he floated through the connecting tunnel and joined Lovell and Haise in the LM.

Aquarius had been created to land on the moon; now it would have to serve as a lifeboat for Lovell, Swigert, and Haise to cross the vast ocean of space, back to Earth. But that wasn't going to be easy, and at the Houston space center, there were soon teams of flight controllers and engineers hard at work figuring out how to make the LM do a job it had never been designed for.

One group had to come up with the precise instructions for firing the lunar module's descent rocket, two hours after Apollo 13 rounded the moon, to send it on the proper course back to Earth. Another team

The crippled service module after its separation from Odyssey.

revived? No one was sure. And so another team was busy figuring out the steps necessary to "wake up" *Odyssey* just before the astronauts reached Earth.

Over the next four days, Ken Mattingly joined in the extraordinary effort to save his former crewmates. Everywhere at the space center—and at aerospace companies all over America, and wherever someone was connected with Apollo—people were in their offices day and night. The back rooms of Mission Control were full of teams working to solve one problem after another. Sometimes they borrowed plans that had been devised for earlier missions but never used. And sometimes they had to invent a brand-new technique.

When *Aquarius* was about to run out of the round canisters used to clean the air of carbon dioxide exhaled by the astronauts—which becomes dangerous if it builds up—they figured out how to use the square canisters from *Odyssey*, even though they were the wrong shape. When the astronauts needed to make a rocket firing to correct their flight path to Earth, the teams in Mission Control found a way to do it without the onboard computer, which had been turned off to save power. Mattingly knew how difficult it must be for Lovell, Swigert, and Haise, so far from home and struggling to survive, having to carry out new techniques they had never practiced, even though they were exhausted and also miserably cold—because the temperature in the powered-down spacecraft didn't get above the forties. But he also knew their frightening ordeal was shared not only by the Apollo "family," but by the people of the world who desperately hoped that the three moon voyagers would make it home alive.

On April 17, Mattingly was in the control center when Lovell and his crew prepared for reentry. Amazingly, they had managed to deal with every problem that had come up so far, even reviving the dead, frozen *Odyssey*. Like everyone else, he waited tensely while the command module made its fiery passage through the

tackled the challenge of conserving the astronauts' precious supplies of electricity, oxygen, and water. *Aquarius* was designed to keep two men alive for forty-five hours, long enough to land on the moon and stay there for thirty-three hours (including two moonwalks) and then link up with the command module in lunar orbit. Now it would have to keep *three* men alive for perhaps twice as long. Inside *Aquarius*, the problem was not oxygen—the lander had more than enough of that for both its own cabin and the attached command module—but electrical power. To use as little power as possible, the astronauts would have to turn off almost every one of the LM's systems.

And then there was *Odyssey* to worry about. Even if Lovell and his crew managed to keep the LM going long enough to reach Earth, they could not reenter the atmosphere in a craft that had no heat shield. They had to use the command module—but by that time, *Odyssey's* systems would have been turned off for almost four days in the frigid cold of space. Could it be

Haise, Swigert, and Lovell aboard the U.S.S. Iwo Jima.

atmosphere. And then, after what seemed like endless minutes of waiting, there was *Odyssey* on the big screen, descending to the waters of the South Pacific under three big, beautiful parachutes. Mission Control erupted in cheers and applause. Soon they could see Lovell, Swigert, and Haise standing on the deck of the recovery ship *Iwo Jima*, waving to the sailors who had picked them up.

They had done it. It would take months to learn that one of the two oxygen tanks inside the service module had exploded, tearing out some of the pipes for the remaining tank. There was hard work ahead; NASA would have to make changes in the spacecraft's design for future missions, to prevent a similar emergency. But just now, everyone could breathe a huge sigh of relief. They had helped three astronauts escape a lonely death in deep space. And they had pulled off an extraordinary group effort that many people, including Mattingly, would call NASA's finest hour.

APOLLO FOURTEEN

JANUARY 31–FEBRUARY 9, 1971

(9 DAYS, 0 HOURS, 2 MINUTES)

COMMANDER: Alan B. Shepard Jr.
COMMAND MODULE PILOT: Stuart A. Roosa
LUNAR MODULE PILOT: Edgar D. Mitchell
OBJECTIVE: Explore the moon's Fra Mauro highlands

FOR ALAN SHEPARD, the most important thing about going to the moon wasn't the chance to visit another world. It was the chance to prove himself. By the time Apollo 14 lifted off with Shepard in command, he had been waiting for that chance for almost ten years.

In May 1961, he'd become the first American in space. It made him a national hero—but what Shepard really wanted was another spaceflight. When the Mercury missions ended in 1963, Shepard was given an assignment the other astronauts envied; he would be commander of the first Gemini mission. But he never got the chance.

Before he could even begin training, Shepard started having dizzy spells. Doctors said he had developed a chronic problem with his inner ear, and they did the worst thing you could possibly do to a pilot: they *grounded* him. Shepard was forbidden to fly in space. He wasn't even allowed to fly an airplane by himself.

Shepard wasn't alone in his ordeal. His fellow Mercury astronaut Donald "Deke" Slayton had also been grounded because of irregular heartbeats. Even though Slayton felt fine and had no problems with flying jets, the doctors said he could not fly in space. Instead, he became the director of Flight Crew Operations at the Houston space center—the astronauts' boss. After

SUNRISE OVER ANTARES (1984): In this view to the east past the Apollo 14 lunar module Antares, the sun is just peeking over the top of the spaceship, making it difficult, even painful, to look that way. It's the same sun we see on Earth, but it appears much brighter because there is no atmosphere on the moon to partially screen its brilliant rays. The sky is painted just the way it looks up there: black. Not a flat black, but a shiny patent-leather black. I could not see stars while walking on the moon, because the sun made the surface so bright. It's a little like walking out on a brightly lit patio and looking up at a dark, clear night sky.

Alan Shepard and Ed Mitchell practice with the Modular Equipment Transporter (MET)—a wheeled cart they will use on the lunar surface—in NASA's reduced gravity training aircraft.

Shepard was grounded, too, Slayton asked his fellow "wounded eagle" to come work for him, and Shepard became the chief astronaut. He helped Slayton with the crucial job of picking the crews for every new space mission. He watched over their training and even rode with them out to the launchpad before their flight. And each time, he wished he were going along.

Finally, in 1968, Shepard secretly went to a surgeon in California who had developed a new kind of operation to fix his ear problem. The surgery was risky—but it worked. By the spring of 1969, he was cleared to fly in space, and he was thrilled when he was named commander of the Apollo 14 mission. Af-

ter the near-disaster of Apollo 13, NASA desperately needed Apollo 14 to be a success. On January 31, 1971, when Shepard lifted off with his crew, rookies Stu Roosa and Ed Mitchell, everyone was painfully aware that another failure might mean the end of the Apollo program.

It didn't take long for problems to start. The men had barely left Earth orbit when there was trouble with the docking system used to attach the nose of the command module *Kitty Hawk* to the top of the lunar module *Antares*. The astronauts tried five times to dock, and each time the ships would not link up. Finally, on the sixth try, using special instructions from Mission Control, the astronauts were able to bring the two craft together. In space and on the ground, everyone breathed a sigh of relief.

Five days later, when Shepard and Mitchell were inside *Antares,* preparing for their descent to the moon, there was another serious problem. This time, it was the electronic circuit for controlling the lunar module's descent engine. In Mission Control, experts realized that when Shepard and Mitchell tried to fire their engine to start their descent, the onboard computer would immediately abort the mission. This time, for help, they turned to the computer experts at the Massachusetts Institute of Technology, who had written the LM's software. They figured out a way for Shepard and Mitchell to work around the problem. Mitchell punched in a long, complicated series of commands on the computer keypad—he couldn't make any mistakes—and it worked! At just the right moment, Shepard and Mitchell lit their descent engine, and *Antares* began heading down to the surface of the moon.

Even then, they weren't out of the woods. Their LM's landing radar, which was supposed to tell them how high they were and how fast they were going, refused to work. Without it, the mission rules were very clear: the landing had to be aborted. But once again, the experts in Mission Control came through. Capcom Fred Haise told Shepard, "Cycle the landing radar circuit breaker." (Translation: Pull out the circuit breaker knob, then push it back in.)

Suddenly, the radar began to work. Now nothing could stop them. Shepard steered *Antares* to a safe landing on the moon's Fra Mauro highlands—the place Apollo 13's Jim Lovell and Fred Haise had planned to go but never reached.

With one foot in a crater, *Antares* tilted to the side, but that wasn't really a problem—after all, Shepard and Mitchell had narrowly escaped losing their mission. Even with all the planning and testing after

Shepard and the MET on the moon—the basis for Alan Bean's cover painting, "Big Al and His Rickshaw."

Apollo 13, this was yet another reminder that in spaceflight things can go wrong in a heartbeat.

A few hours later, Shepard finally climbed down the lunar module's ladder and set foot on the ancient lunar dust. His words ended ten frustrating years of waiting: "It's been a long way, but we're here."

Then something happened that caught him completely by surprise. High overhead in the black lunar sky, he spotted the Earth, a brilliant, glowing crescent. Looking at it, Shepard was suddenly overwhelmed by the beauty of his home world, and his own relief at finally reaching his goal. Inside his helmet, Shepard—known as a tough, even icy character—found tears streaming down his face. After a few moments he got control of his emotions and got his mind back on the job. It was time for him and Mitchell to explore the Fra Mauro highlands.

THE NEXT DAY, with one successful moonwalk behind them—they'd set up scientific experiments and

AFTER THEY CAME home from the moon, Alan Shepard, Stu Roosa, and Ed Mitchell couldn't kiss their wives and children. They couldn't go to postflight parties with their colleagues at NASA. Like the two lunar landing crews before them, they were in quarantine, which lasted until twenty-one days after Shepard and Mitchell's departure from the surface of the moon. That practice was started during planning for Apollo 11, when NASA knew that Neil Armstrong and his crew would be the first humans to come in contact with lunar dust. Some people feared that there might be living organisms in that dust, and that the astronauts might carry those organisms back to Earth with them. In the darkest possibility, maybe the "moon germs" would create a plague on Earth for which humans had no natural defenses.

Of course, most scientists knew this was extremely unlikely, to say the least. After all, the moon has no air or water to support any kind of life. Its surface is exposed to fierce heat and cold and to deadly radiation from the sun and other stars. So how could there be anything alive on the moon? Still, no one could be *absolutely sure*, until someone actually went there, that there were no "moon germs." And so, when Neil Armstrong, Mike Collins, and Buzz Aldrin splashed down, their command module was met by swimmers wearing special biological isolation garments (BIGs). First they scrubbed the outside of the command module with disinfectant. Then they opened the hatch just long enough to toss in a set of BIGs for the astronauts. When Armstrong and his crew emerged into the life raft, they looked like space aliens themselves! After arriving on the recovery ship, the U.S.S. *Hornet*, they walked to a special trailer, where they and a doctor were sealed inside. The men took off their BIGs, showered, put on normal flying coveralls, and settled in for the

Sealed inside a Mobile Quarantine Facility, the Apollo 14 crew (left to right: Roosa, Shepard, Mitchell) greet the press and the crew of the U.S.S. New Orleans, February 1971.

trip back to Houston. At the space center, the astronauts spent the rest of their twenty-one-day quarantine inside the same sealed facility where the moon rocks were kept.

As most people expected, Armstrong's crew didn't get sick. And scientists' testing of the lunar rock and dust samples confirmed that there was nothing alive in them. Still, just to be extra safe, NASA kept the quarantine going through Apollo 14 (although the astronauts no longer had to wear BIGs when they got out of the spacecraft, just a respirator that covered their faces). With Apollo 15, NASA ended the practice for returning moon voyagers.

The lunar rock and dust samples are another story: most of them are kept in isolation in special laboratories— not because anyone is afraid they might harm humans, but to keep the precious samples from being affected by exposure to the Earth's atmosphere.

done a bit of exploring—Shepard and Mitchell once again emerged from *Antares*. This time, the goal was to reach the rim of Cone Crater, which was almost a mile away, farther than any previous moonwalkers had traveled—and they had to get there on foot.

There, at the edge of this 1,200-foot-diameter pit, scientists had told them they would find some of the oldest rocks on the moon. To get there, the men had to climb up the side of a broad ridge that rose 300 feet above the surrounding plains. They soon found that the climb was much harder than anyone expected.

For one thing, walking up such a steep slope in a space suit was very, very tiring. The normal motions you make climbing a hill—bending your leg at the knee and at the hip—were almost impossible. To make it even harder, the two astronauts had taken along a new device that was supposed to help them, a two-wheeled cart loaded with rock-collecting tools, cameras, maps, and the rock samples they'd already picked up. They had to take turns pulling it up the hill, trying to keep it from turning over every time it hit a rock or a bump in the low gravity.

And there was an even bigger problem: they didn't know where they were.

They had a photomap marked with craters and other landmarks along the way, and they'd studied it before the flight. On the moon, though, it was almost impossible to figure out. Each time they topped a ridge, expecting to see the rim of the giant crater, they saw only more ridges, more rocks. They spent most of an hour searching. In the end, with time and oxygen running short, the disappointed explorers had to call off their search for Cone's rim. There was just

enough time to gather a few rock samples from the top of the ridge before the long walk back to the LM.

Happily, they found it much easier coming down, running in long, flying leaps, with the tool cart bouncing along behind them. And when they returned to *Antares*, they knew that with all the problems, they'd still accomplished most of the mission's goals.

But Shepard had one more personal task that wasn't on the flight plan, something he'd thought of back on Earth, during training.

Now, standing before the TV camera, he pulled a golf ball out of his space suit pocket and said, "In my left hand, I have a little white pellet that's familiar to millions of Americans." He'd made a makeshift golf club, using the head of a six iron attached to his rock-collection-tool handle. In his pressurized suit he couldn't bring his arms together the way he would have if he were playing golf on Earth, and he had to swing with one hand. But after a couple of tries, Shepard connected with the ball, which went sailing away in the moon's one-sixth gravity. "Miles and miles!" he announced proudly to a listening world. Alan Shepard had become the first lunar golfer, and no one minded if he exaggerated just a little.

He'd earned it.

SHEPARD AND MITCHELL *would be the last team of Apollo moonwalkers to struggle with navigating on the moon. Only three Apollo missions remained, but they would include something amazing: A battery powered car called the lunar rover with its own navigation system. With it, the astronauts of Apollos 15, 16, and 17 would raise Apollo to new heights of discovery, in some of the most spectacular places ever visited on the moon.*

(OVERLEAF) IN FLIGHT (1990): *As Apollo 14 astronauts Alan Shepard and Edgar Mitchell were winding up their second moonwalk, Al turned toward the television camera. "Houston, you might recognize what I have in my right hand as the handle for the contingency sample collector. It just happens to have a genuine six iron attached to the end. . . ." Al would say later, "The fun with the golf shot certainly had to be the greatest thrill."*

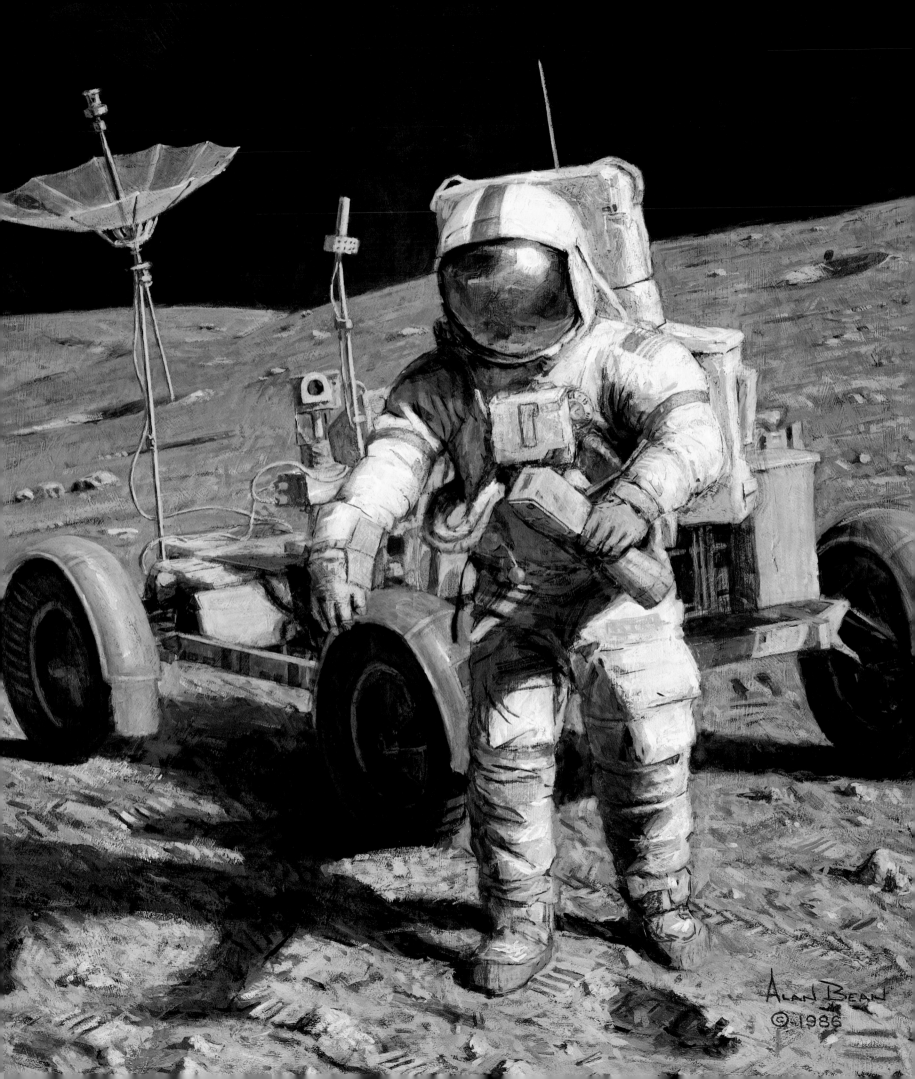

APOLLO FIFTEEN

JULY 26 – AUGUST 7, 1971

(12 DAYS, 7 HOURS, 11 MINUTES, 53 SECONDS)

COMMANDER: David R. Scott
COMMAND MODULE PILOT: Alfred M. Worden
LUNAR MODULE PILOT: James B. Irwin
OBJECTIVE: First extended scientific expedition to the moon

JIM IRWIN GOT two surprises when he climbed off the lunar rover and stood on the side of a lunar mountain called Hadley Delta. One was the steepness of the slope—it was much greater than he'd realized while riding the rover—and the other was the view. Standing here, 300 feet above the floor of a broad valley, he and his commander, Dave Scott, gazed out at a truly stunning sight. The valley floor was covered with enormous craters, and on some of them they could see huge boulders. To the west, far in the distance, a giant, winding canyon called Hadley Rille—4,900 feet wide and 1,300 feet deep—sliced through the plains; they would drive to its rim to-morrow, on their third exploration. But for Irwin, the best part of this awesome view was the mountains. All along the horizon, he saw the great peaks of the moon's Apennine Range ascending into the black sky. It was funny; on the moon, with no trees or telephone poles to judge size and distance, you couldn't really tell how high those mountains were. But Irwin knew they were very high indeed—the tallest, Mount Hadley, stood 15,000 feet above the valley floor. Because there was no air—and there-fore, no haze—everything looked incredibly clear. And it was all absolutely still, just as it had been for countless millions of years.

TELEPHOTO OPPORTUNITY (1986): Dave Scott is shown heading our way with camera in hand. We can tell it's Dave because the Apollo 15 Commander has red stripes on his suit and helmet. He and Jim Irwin have just parked their lunar rover near the lip of Hadley Rille, and Dave is planning to take some detailed photos of the far wall of the gorge. The remote controlled television camera looks our way, beaming its signal back to Earth, some 240,000 miles above us.

The Apollo 15 crew and the lunar rover. Left to right: Irwin, Scott, Worden.

As a man who had loved the mountains all his life, Irwin felt lucky to be one of the first two people to visit the mountains of the moon. He knew that was possible only because of all of the new advances on Apollo 15.

The improved suits and backpacks he and Scott were wearing carried enough oxygen and cooling water for a moonwalk lasting seven hours—a full working day on the surface of another world. Their lunar module *Falcon* was loaded with extra oxygen, water, and food, so they could stay on the moon for three full days and take three moonwalks.

And, for the first time on any mission, they'd brought along their own car—how American could you get!—the battery-powered lunar rover. It had made the journey from Earth folded up and attached to the side of the lunar module, and they'd unloaded it yesterday, during their first moonwalk. It was really more like a separate spacecraft, with its own radio and navigation system. It had wheels made of woven piano wire to give it the best grip on the moon's powdery surface. And it worked beautifully. It was amazing how easily the rover had driven up this steep slope. But to *walk* up it—that was something else. The mountainside was covered with a soft, thick layer of dust, and each time Irwin took a step, his feet sank

(OVERLEAF) *CEREMONY ON THE PLAIN AT HADLEY (1983): Before Dave Scott and Jim Irwin started their exploration, they had to attend to a matter of ceremony. Planting the flag is a tradition in exploration, and moon exploration was no exception. They couldn't, however, count on the wind blowing out the flag, since there is no air on the moon. So there is a small metal snap-up curtain rod along the top edge of the flag to hold it out.*

FOR ANYONE BACK on Earth, some of the most exciting moments of the Apollo lunar missions came when you could turn on the TV and see the words *Live from the Moon.*

Those words had appeared on screens around the world for the first time as Neil Armstrong prepared to take his first steps onto the Sea of Tranquility. A small black-and-white camera, mounted on an equipment tray on the side of the lunar module's descent stage, broadcast Armstrong and Aldrin's moonwalk to Earth. The pictures were nowhere near the quality that viewers were used to, but that hardly mattered—there was live TV from the moon!

And by Apollo 12, the pictures had improved, thanks to a color camera. Unfortunately, the camera failed early in the mission's first moonwalk when Alan Bean accidentally pointed it at the sun for a moment too long, burning out the camera's light sensor. Color TV was back on the moon for Apollo 14, although its view was limited; the camera had to be connected to the lunar module by a long cable, so the astronauts couldn't carry it with them as they explored. As Alan Shepard and Ed Mitchell headed away from their lunar module *Antares* to climb Cone Crater, they were soon too far away to be seen. However, when they returned, the camera broadcast Shepard's lunar golf shot to the world.

Things improved greatly for the final three Apollo landings, which carried the battery-powered lunar rover. With its own communications system, the rover could broadcast its own TV pictures directly to Earth. A new, higher-quality color camera was mounted at the front of the rover, equipped with a zoom lens. On Earth, engineer Ed Fendell controlled the camera from his console in Mission Control. He could turn the camera to the left or right, tilt it up or down, and zoom the picture in or out. That was especially important to the scientists who were following the astronauts' work from a back room in Mission Control. The TV camera gave them detailed views of the landscape, and it let them look over the astronauts' shoulders as they collected samples. If they spotted a particularly interesting looking rock, they could even ask the moonwalkers to pick it up for them.

For everyone else who tuned in, the spectacular pictures from the rover were a chance to witness the most extraordinary explorations in history. There were views of the astronauts bouncing in the moon's one-sixth gravity, and of spectacular mountains, craters, and boulders.

When Ed Fendell pointed the camera at a blue-and-white world high overhead, the people of Earth could see themselves from a quarter-million miles out in space. And when the astronauts left the moon, leaving their rover behind, there was one more special TV shot: the camera broadcast the lunar module ascent stage rocketing off the surface of the moon and receding into the black sky as it headed for lunar orbit.

Broadcast to Earth on live TV, Dave Scott takes his first steps onto the moon on July 31, 1971.

into the powder. It felt like trying to walk up a sand dune. They could never have gotten to this high place without the rover. Scott even said, "Man, I'd sure hate to have to climb up here!" Irwin couldn't have agreed more.

Still, riding the rover was quite an adventure. It could reach a top speed of eight miles an hour, which may sound slow, but it felt fast enough when you were riding it. In the moon's one-sixth gravity, the rover would sail into space for a long moment each time it hit a rock or a bump. It was a little like being in a rowboat on a choppy sea, but the motions were sharper, since the moon was much harder. Scott and Irwin were wearing seat belts—and they needed them.

Because their time on the moon was so precious, Scott always drove as fast as he could, and sometimes he had to swerve suddenly to avoid a boulder or a crater, telling Irwin, "Hang on!" There were a couple

of times, bouncing along the mountainside, when Irwin actually worried that the rover might turn over, but that never did happen. (Of course if it had, in the low gravity the rover was so light they could have just picked it up and turned it right side up again.)

Even when they were stopped, there were moments of surprise: Once, while Scott was taking pictures of a boulder on the steep slope, the rover began to slide downhill, and Irwin had to grab it and hold on so it wouldn't get away from them. And there was always the chance that the rover might break down. If that happened, he and Scott would have to walk all the way back to *Falcon*, which was now more than three miles away. He could see it out on the plains, a tiny speck in this alien wilderness.

But right now, the two men weren't thinking about what could go wrong. They were excited about all the things that were going *right*. And, even more impor-

tant, they were eager to find out what the mountains of the moon were made of—and so were the geologists back on Earth who had trained them.

These geologists, who studied rocks to figure out the history of a planet, were eagerly following Scott and Irwin's activities from a back room in Mission Control, thanks to the rover's color TV camera, which was controlled from Earth. For months before the flight, they'd led the astronauts through some lunar-like terrain: the lava flows of Hawaii, a steep-sided canyon in New Mexico, and rugged slopes high in the Rocky Mountains of Colorado. On these trips, Scott and Irwin learned to recognize types of rocks they might find on the moon, including a white-colored rock called anorthosite, which scientists believed was the main rock type in the oldest part of the moon's crust. If the astronauts could bring home a piece of this ancient crust, scientists would be able to look back farther into the moon's past than ever before—maybe even to the time of its birth. They'd told the astronauts they might find pieces of anorthosite on the slopes of the mountain called Hadley Delta.

Just now, on the mountain, the astronauts arrived at the third of several planned stops on this moon-

HADLEY RILLE (1996): Hadley Rille was perhaps one of the most visually exciting feature visited on any of the six lunar landing missions. Canyon-like, it meanders almost 70 miles across the lunar surface. From our point of view looking north, we can see the sunlit far wall of the rille as it moves left to right just beyond Apollo 15 astronauts Dave Scott and Jim Irwin. It then turns northwest to disappear in the distance, its east wall in shadow. Dave had reported when they first drove up in the rover, "Man, you ought to have a great view on your TV. This is unreal! The most beautiful thing I've ever seen."

LEFT: Dave Scott looking at the Genesis Rock in the Houston Lunar Receiving Lab. RIGHT: The rock shown in close-up.

walk, a football field–size crater called Spur (as they had with all the features they visited, the astronauts had named it before the flight). The geologists had told them that the rims of craters were great places to hunt for interesting samples, and one rock along Spur's edge caught Irwin's eye. It was different from any other he and Scott had seen. It was completely white, and it was sitting on a little mound of dust, as if someone had put it there for them to pick up. After they collected it with a special pair of tongs and held it in their hands and saw it up close, they realized they had discovered something very special. "Guess what we just found," said Scott. *"Guess what we just found!"* Irwin heard the excitement in his commander's voice and smiled. Scott continued, "I think we found what we came for." It was a chunk of anorthosite—a piece of the moon's original crust.

After Scott and Irwin were back on Earth, scientists would analyze the rock and would learn that it was 4.5 billion years old—almost as old as the moon itself! It was more than half a billion years older than any moon rock brought back before. This special rock, which would help scientists unravel the mysteries of the moon's origin, became known as the Genesis Rock.

Scott and Irwin wouldn't have minded spending the entire moonwalk at Spur Crater, hunting for geologic treasure. But they knew they couldn't do that. Mission Control, always thinking about the astronauts' oxygen supply, told Scott and Irwin to start driving back down the mountain and head for *Falcon*. That was the most frustrating thing about being a lunar explorer: there was never enough time.

THE SPIRIT OF EXPLORATION (1995): This is Dave Scott with his Hasselblad camera. He and Jim Irwin were on the surface of the moon at a site rich with scientific potential. As I watched Dave and Jim go about their work, I was impressed. We had come so far so fast. Only two years earlier the whole world had watched the black-and-white television pictures of Neil Armstrong and Buzz Aldrin on the moon, but the two of them had never ventured far from their lunar module. Now, on beautiful computer-enhanced color television, Dave and Jim explored five times the surface area of the three previous landings put together. It was a stunning achievement.

APOLLO SIXTEEN

APRIL 16-27, 1972

(11 DAYS, 1 HOUR, 51 MINUTES, 5 SECONDS)

COMMANDER: John W. Young
COMMAND MODULE PILOT: T. Kenneth Mattingly II
LUNAR MODULE PILOT: Charles M. Duke Jr.
OBJECTIVE: First mission to the moon's central highlands

EVERY TWO HOURS Ken Mattingly circled the moon alone, flying through brilliant sunlight, then soft earthlight, and then star-sprayed night. Below him, filling the windows, was a desolate and pockmarked panorama. For forty-five minutes out of each orbit, flying over the lunar far side, he was cut off from all communications with Earth. During that time he was completely and utterly alone. But he was never lonely. In fact, he loved the experience.

Six years after being selected as an astronaut, and two years after being bumped from the crew of Apollo 13 at the last minute by a nonexistent case of German measles, Ken Mattingly had made it to the moon. And now, with the Apollo 16 command module *Casper* all to himself while his crewmates explored the surface, he was having the time of his life.

If you had asked Ken Mattingly what he most wanted, before he was chosen for an Apollo mission, his answer would have been simple. Like most astronauts, he wanted to walk on the moon. But when he was named as the command module pilot on John Young's Apollo crew, he knew that would never happen. Oh, if there had been several more moon landings, he probably would have gone on to be a mission com-

ON THE RIM (1986): Apollo 16 astronauts John Young and Charlie Duke have just arrived on the rim of North Ray Crater. John is on the left selecting tools, while Charlie is removing the Hasselblad camera with the 500-millimeter telephoto lens from beneath the seat. Charlie would later report, "We did take the photos of the interior of the crater. I couldn't see the bottom and I wasn't going to get close enough to see in, because there was no way I could have gotten out if I had fallen in." North Ray was the largest crater—300 feet in diameter—and deepest crater—who knows how deep—directly explored in the Apollo program.

LEFT: Duke and Young during geology training. RIGHT: Young (center) and Duke (foreground) inspect the lunar rover.

mander, and then he would have gotten his chance. But after the first landing, public interest in Apollo had fallen off sharply, and NASA's budget had been cut. There wasn't enough money to keep Apollo going indefinitely, not if they wanted to do other things besides going to the moon, like building a permanent space station in Earth orbit. NASA had canceled the last three planned landings, Apollos 18, 19, and 20. After Apollo 16, there would be only one more lunar mission.

And so Ken Mattingly was happy to accept his role as the "truck driver" of the Apollo 16 mission. That was his job: get John Young and Charlie Duke into lunar orbit so they could go ahead and land, and then, when they returned from the surface, take them back home again. He'd trained for that role as hard as any other command module pilot, becoming an expert on his spacecraft's systems and learning how to navigate to and from the moon. And while Young and Duke were on the surface, he was just as happy to use his special training as a scientific observer of the moon from orbit. He didn't pretend to be in love with science, but still, he found it fascinating work. And if he could help the geologists solve a few lunar mysteries, he would be glad to do it.

But he almost didn't get the chance. A couple

MOONROCK—EARTHBOUND (1984): Collecting moon rocks was more than just reaching down and grabbing ones we happened to like. The first problem was knowing which rocks were worth the time and energy. That's why we had six years of geologic training before going to the moon. The first rock we were taught to select at a site was one that looked most like all the other rocks in the area. The "typical" rock and its immediate surrounding area were photographed before we disturbed anything. Here John Young is using the long tweezer-like tongs at a site near where the LM Orion has landed. Charlie Duke will inspect the rock, making specific comments to the geologists on Earth, and then place it in a numbered sample bag.

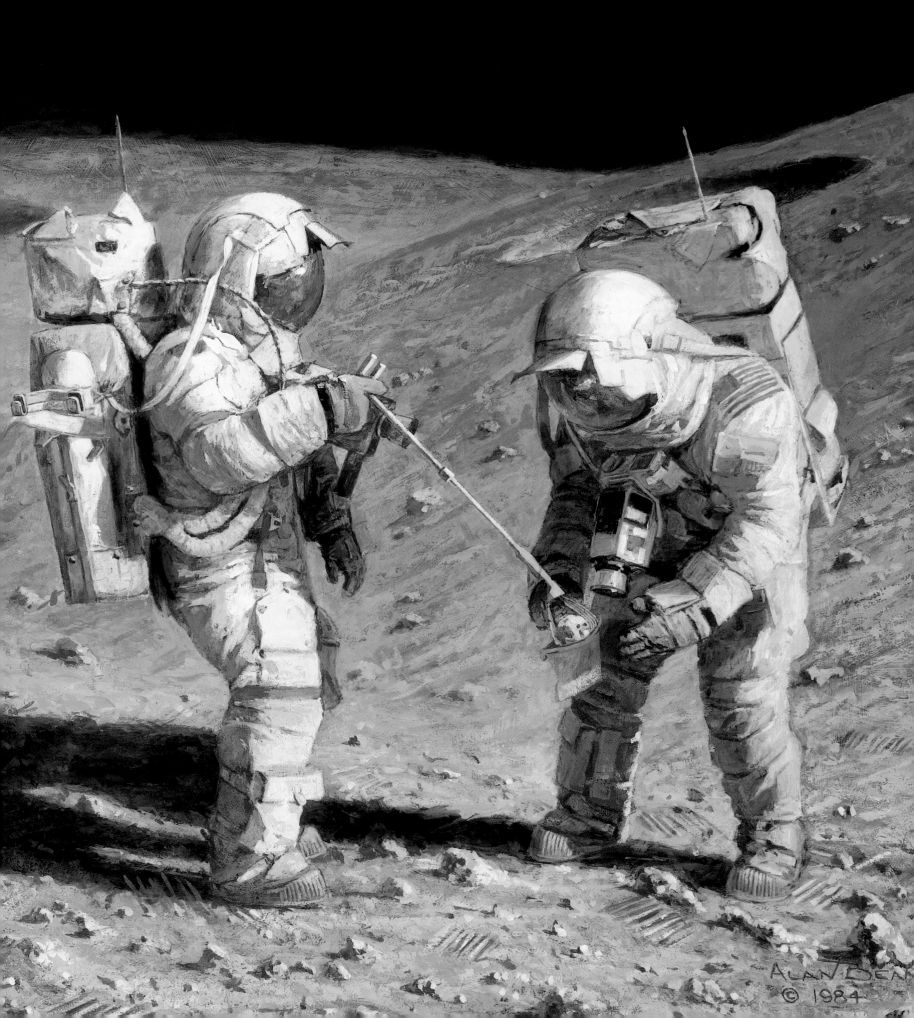

of hours before their scheduled landing, Young and Duke were flying free in the lunar module *Orion*, leaving Mattingly alone in *Casper*. The next step was for Mattingly to briefly fire his service module's big rocket engine to adjust his orbit. But when he was getting ready, he discovered there was a serious problem: when he tried to point the engine nozzle for the firing, it shook badly. The shaking only happened when he used a backup pointing system—the main system was okay—but still, everyone was worried.

For six hours, while Mission Control studied the problem, the landing was postponed. They told Mattingly to fly *Casper* close to *Orion*, in case they had to link up and head back to Earth, maybe even using the lunar module's engine. It was a depressing six hours—all three astronauts were sure their mission was over.

But after all that time circling the moon, waiting anxiously, they heard capcom Jim Irwin say that the experts in Mission Control thought it wasn't a serious problem, after all. The mission could continue! And when Young and Duke flew *Orion* down to a safe land-

Ken Mattingly making notes in his flight checklist during a practice countdown, March 31, 1972.

LIKE ALL MOONWALKERS, Charlie

Duke spent much of his time on the moon's surface picking up rock and dust samples to bring home to the scientists on Earth. But he also left something behind, something very personal. It was a photograph of himself and his family taken before the mission. On the back, he'd written: *This is the family of astronaut Charles M. Duke.* He'd carried the photo to the moon in the pocket of his space suit, and when he had a free moment, he pulled it out and left it in the dust of the Descartes highlands.

The photo is still there, along with a variety of other items left by the six teams of Apollo moonwalkers. There is a small aluminum sculpture of a fallen astronaut, left by Apollo 15 commander Dave Scott, along with a small plaque bearing the names of the astronauts and cosmonauts who had lost their lives in the effort to explore space. Alan Shepard left a couple of golf balls. And after he parked his lunar rover for the last time, Dave Scott placed a Bible on its control panel—because if anyone visited the Apollo 15 landing site sometime in the future, he wanted them to know a little bit about the human beings who first landed there in 1971.

If you went back to the six Apollo landing sites today, you'd find a number of other things, large and small, that the astronauts left behind. There are the six lunar module descent stages, which served as the astronauts' launching platforms when they returned to lunar orbit. There are six American flags. You'd find six sets of scientific experiments, and various tools left over from the moonwalks. There are twelve backpacks, discarded by the moonwalkers after they returned to the lunar module cabin.

And something else, too numerous to count: footprints. Those footprints, bearing the impression of the treads on the astronauts' boots, are perhaps the

The Duke family photo on the lunar surface.

Paul Van Hoeydonck's Fallen Astronaut, the only piece of art on the moon, and a memorial plaque, both left by Apollo 15's Dave Scott.

most meaningful things the moonwalkers left behind. They show that human beings had the courage and ingenuity to leave their home world to explore another celestial body. And because there is nothing on the airless moon to erase them, except for the slow sandblasting by micrometeorites, those footprints could last for a million years.

ing on the moon's Descartes Highlands, Mattingly was just about as relieved as they were. He knew how long and hard they had trained to visit the moon's central highlands. Over the radio, Mattingly could hear Duke's Southern drawl, full of joy, just after touchdown: "Wowwww! Whoa, man! Old *Orion* is finally here, Houston! Fan*tas*tic!"

After that, Mattingly turned to his own solo mission. He had his own flight plan, his own photographs to take, his own experiments to conduct. He even had his own separate radio channel with Mission Control. And although he wasn't hearing Young and Duke's voices over the radio, he could just imagine what a marvelous time they must be having as they explored the Descartes Highlands.

But, honestly, he couldn't imagine how bounding across the lunar surface could possibly be more fun than orbiting the moon *by yourself*. Nothing compared with the feeling of floating inside the command module, gliding silently over the craters. He could even turn on the portable tape player and listen to classical music (which he liked much better than the country music Young and Duke brought along). As a fighter pilot, he'd always flown jets that had only one seat; he'd had no one to answer to but himself. And now, inside *Casper*, it was the same—only it was even more thrilling.

And then there was the moon.

Before the flight, Mattingly had worked closely

THE MAXIMUM PUSH—CHARLIE DUKE, SOIL SCIENTIST (1993): Charlie Duke is giving a maximum push to his self-recording penetrometer. The cone and shaft penetrate the lunar soil, recording the force and the depth. The recorder will be brought back to Earth to help scientists better understand the mechanical properties of the lunar soil. Charlie's maximum push is not without complications. He will shortly lose his balance and fall to the lunar surface. But not to worry! With no damage except for getting a little dusty, he will be able to do a simple push up to his knees, then a quick knee hop back to his feet.

with the scientists, studying the craters, mountains, and other features he would be able to see. And now that he was here, he was amazed at how much detail he really *could* see. To someone who had never studied it, the moon might look like it was all the same, but in reality, it was full of variety. Each region held a different story of the moon's past. There were tales of powerful meteorite impacts that had blasted out huge craters, and ancient eruptions of glowing lava that had poured out onto the landscape, cooling into vast plains of volcanic rock. There were enough mysteries to keep the scientists busy for the rest of their lives.

And from what he could tell, Young and Duke were uncovering their own mysteries, down on the surface. Every so often he would ask Mission Control how they were doing, and he was told they were finding lots of surprises. Instead of volcanic rocks, as the scientists had predicted, they were finding rocks that had been formed by the violence of meteorite impacts. Soon enough, they would be back in lunar orbit, bringing with them their haul of lunar rocks and dust, each sample with its own story. And if those weren't the stories everyone was expecting, Mattingly knew, that was just fine. After all, the whole point of being an explorer was to discover what was *really* there, whatever it turned out to be.

DOCUMENTING THE SAMPLE (1985): When we found an interesting rock on the moon, we couldn't just grab it and put it in a bag. In order to make sure that they brought back scientifically useful samples, John Young and Charlie Duke worked as a team. Charlie took two photographs of the sample area. John or Charlie picked up the sample, examined it carefully, and reported any special observations to Earth before placing it in a numbered sample bag; then, another photo of the site, and they moved on. A simple procedure, but the results were enormous. Here we see John, who has placed the gnomon (which casts a shadow to help scientists back on Earth accurately determine the orientation of the rock) near the selected sample and stepped back so Charlie can take a picture.

APOLLO SEVENTEEN

DECEMBER 7-19, 1972

(12 DAYS, 13 HOURS, 51 MINUTES, 59 SECONDS)

COMMANDER: Eugene A. Cernan
COMMAND MODULE PILOT: Ronald E. Evans
LUNAR MODULE PILOT: Harrison H. "Jack" Schmitt
OBJECTIVE: Explore the moon's Taurus-Littrow valley

SEEN FROM EARTH, *the moon looked no different on the night of December 13, 1972, than it had for all of human history. Even with the most powerful telescope in existence, no evidence could be seen that at that moment, two men were living and working there. But to the scientists, engineers, managers, and astronauts of Project Apollo, the moon had changed forever. Because of their dedication, their ingenuity, and their hard work, the moon was now no longer just a light in the sky; it was a place. A place you could go to. But on this December night, everyone at NASA knew something wonderful was about to end. Apollo's final moonwalk was under way.*

GENE CERNAN STOOD on the steep slope of the mountain called the North Massif and stole a moment to take in the view. His space suit, once clean and white, was now filthy—because it was covered with moon dust. For the last three days, he and his lunar module pilot, geologist-astronaut Jack Schmitt, had been exploring a valley near the crater Littrow, at the southeastern edge of the moon's Sea of Serenity. That valley, ringed by the steep-sided Taurus Mountains, had turned out to be one of the most spectacular places ever visited by human beings.

For scientists back on Earth, who could hardly wait

MANKIND ROCK (1994): This is Gene Cernan near the end of the third moonwalk of Apollo 17. He and Jack Schmitt had completed most of their work and were just gathering final equipment and samples. Gene turned toward the television camera and said, "Jack has picked up a very significant rock, composed of many fragments . . . probably from all parts of the moon, probably billions of years old, but a rock of all sizes and shapes and even colors that had grown together to become a cohesive rock, outlasting the nature of space, sort of living together in a very coherent, very peaceful manner. We'd like to share a piece of this rock with many of the countries throughout the world. We hope that this will be a symbol of what our feelings are."

for the rocks he and Schmitt were now collecting, the valley of Taurus-Littrow offered one more chance to probe the secrets of the moon's birth and history.

And for Cernan, it was the high point of a long and amazing journey. More than three years after coming within nine miles of the moon on Apollo 10, he had finally made it down those last 50,000 feet to the surface. He had left his own footprints in the ancient lunar dust. And just as important, to Cernan, he had done it as mission commander. If he had stayed in the navy as a fighter pilot, he would have wanted to lead a squadron of jets. As an astronaut, his ultimate goal had been to command an Apollo lunar landing crew. For Cernan, this was truly the top of the mountain.

Cernan could hardly believe the journey he had taken to get here. For the second time, he had ridden a giant Saturn V rocket off the Earth. For the second time, he had seen his home world shrink to the size

★ THE MOON ROCKS ★

(AND WHAT HAPPENED TO THEM AFTER THEY GOT TO EARTH)

WHEN THE APOLLO 17 command module splashed down in the Pacific, it was filled with scientific treasure: the 243 pounds of moon rocks and dust that had been collected by Gene Cernan and Jack Schmitt in the valley of Taurus-Littrow. Like the samples from the previous five landings, these were carried to Earth in special aluminum "rock boxes" that looked like small, silvery suitcases. To protect the samples from exposure to Earth's atmosphere, the astronauts had sealed the boxes while they were standing on the moon, in the vacuum of space.

When the rock boxes first reached Houston, they were taken to a special Lunar Receiving Laboratory at the space center and placed in vacuum chambers that actually had space suit arms and gloves attached to their sides. Reaching in with the gloves, technicians opened the containers and removed the rocks. As you can imagine, working this way was difficult and tiring. Eventually, scientists realized that lunar rocks and dust would not be harmed by pure nitrogen, and they transferred the samples to cabinets filled with this gas, at normal pressure. These cabinets had long, flexible rubber gloves attached to their sides, which made it much easier for scientists to work on the samples.

With each new Apollo landing, more and more samples arrived in Houston. By the time the Apollo 17 rocks and dust arrived, the total came to 842 pounds.

Today, most of the samples are kept at the Houston space center in a special vault built to withstand hurricanes, which are common in that part of the country. Just to be extra careful, a portion of the collection is kept at a NASA facility in New Mexico.

Protecting the lunar treasures also means only certain materials are allowed to touch them, to avoid contamination. All the tools used in the sample vaults are made of aluminum, stainless steel, or Teflon. When they need to pick up a rock by hand, technicians use gloves made of Teflon. Samples are stored inside Teflon bags or in containers made of aluminum or stainless steel.

The samples are managed by curators, like those at an art museum, who know the locations of every chip of rock, every vial of dust. When scientists around the world study the lunar samples, they work with very small quantities, because their instruments are so sensitive that they usually don't need more than that. And most of the samples are rarely touched at all, preserved so that the scientists of tomorrow will be able to use even more powerful methods and instruments to study them.

Jack Schmitt uses a long-handled scoop to collect samples at Taurus-Littrow.

of his outstretched thumb. He'd made his second trip into lunar orbit, to gaze down at a bleak, cratered world. It was all just as spectacular as the first time. And *this* time, he and Schmitt had gone into their lunar module *Challenger* and separated from Ron Evans in the command module *America*, and he'd steered that lunar module to a landing on the moon.

Before the flight, he and Schmitt had promised themselves that Apollo 17, the final lunar voyage, would be the pinnacle of the entire program. He'd told the workers who were testing his spacecraft, "This may be our last, but let's make it our best." And those workers—like the rest of the thousands of people whose efforts made Apollo possible—had done their jobs superbly. They had helped him and Schmitt get to this spectacular place, the valley of Taurus-Littrow.

Now, on the moon, he and Schmitt had driven farther, collected more rocks, and taken more photographs than any astronauts before them. They had even driven their lunar rover up onto the side of this mountain, where they took rock samples from a boulder the size of a house. For the scientists back on Earth, it

TRACY'S BOULDER (1984): Gene Cernan and Jack Schmitt have finished their work at Station Six and are loading the lunar rover with their samples and experiments. When I showed this painting to Gene, he said he wished he had thought of writing his daughter's name in the dust, but the idea didn't come until he got back home. It was so appealing that I gave him a blank sheet of paper and asked him to write Tracy's name the way he would have wanted it in the dust on the moon. Then I got to work with my paintbrushes.

(OVERLEAF) THE LAST MAN ON THE MOON (1993): It is December 14, 1972. Commander Eugene Cernan is the last human being to stand on the surface of the moon. There are a total of twelve of us who got to explore another world as representatives of the people of the United States of America. There are only six flags on the moon, and all of them are the Stars and Stripes. We did it by working together. Landing men on the moon and returning safely to Earth was a brilliant triumph of the human spirit.

Ron Evans during his spacewalk, retrieving film canisters from the service module as America heads back to Earth, December 17, 1972.

was like Christmas morning—especially because Jack Schmitt was one of their own, a professional geologist as well as an astronaut. Having Schmitt on the moon was almost as good as getting to go themselves.

Now, while Schmitt gathered samples, Cernan took a moment to look out over the valley. Far in the distance, he spotted his lunar module, *Challenger*, a tiny dot in this ancient wilderness.

He'd never been so far out on a limb. So many things would have to go right for him and his crewmates to get home safely. The rover would have to keep working, or he and Schmitt would have to walk back three and a half miles to the safety of their LM. A few hours from now, *Challenger*'s ascent engine would have to fire, or they would die on the moon. And if they made it back to the command module and rejoined his old friend Ron Evans, they still weren't out of danger, not by a long shot. In a few days, *America*'s rocket engine would also have to work, or they would never get out of lunar orbit. Then, when they reached the

Earth, traveling at 25,000 miles per hour, they would have to hit the atmosphere at *just* the right angle. If they came in too steeply, they would burn up. If they came in too shallow, they would bounce right off the atmosphere and out into space forever. And even if they made it through the fiery reentry, when temperatures just outside the command module would soar to thousands of degrees Fahrenheit because of friction with the atmosphere, there was one more hurdle: the parachutes would have to open, slowing the command module to a safe splashdown in the Pacific, or else the impact would kill them.

AMAZINGLY, ALL OF those crucial steps along the path to the moon and back worked for Cernan and his crew, just as they had on almost every mission in the Apollo program. As they stood on the deck of their recovery ship, the aircraft carrier U.S.S. *Ticonderoga*, they felt proud of their mission. For the rest of their lives, they would cherish the honor of being among the twenty-four humans to leave Earth and visit another world. But they also knew they stood on the shoulders of giants: the visionary physicist Robert Goddard, inventor of the liquid-fuel rocket engine; Wernher von Braun, who made liquid-fuel rockets a practical reality and went on to create the giant Saturn V; Russian schoolteacher Konstantin Tsiolkovsky, who'd thought out the techniques necessary for a lunar voyage at the start of the twentieth century—decades before the space age. The list went all the way back to geniuses of centuries past, including German astronomer Johannes Kepler, who first described the motions of planets around the sun, and England's Isaac Newton, whose theory of gravity and laws of motion are the foundation of spaceflight. And, most of all, they knew there were 400,000 dedicated people who had been working night and day for a decade to make Apollo a success.

WHAT A GREAT WAY TO START HOME (1983): The shapes of the lunar module are interesting to look at and they were fun to paint. Challenger *has the look of a machine built to do a specific thing well and efficiently. This was all-important to Gene Cernan and Jack Schmitt because if, for example, the rocket engine we see at the bottom did not do its job, they would never come home. I remember that on Apollo 12, when we had rocketed back into lunar orbit and were going fast again, I felt we were really going to make it. It was a great way to start home.*

Now that great adventure was over. Days before, Cernan had tried to express his feelings about the end of Apollo before taking the last human footsteps on the moon and climbing back into the LM. "As I take man's last step from the surface, back home for some time to come—but we believe not too long into the future—I'd like to just say what I believe history will record: that America's challenge of today has forged man's destiny of tomorrow. And, as we leave the moon at Taurus-Littrow, we leave as we came and, God willing, as we shall return, with peace and hope for all mankind. Godspeed the crew of Apollo 17."

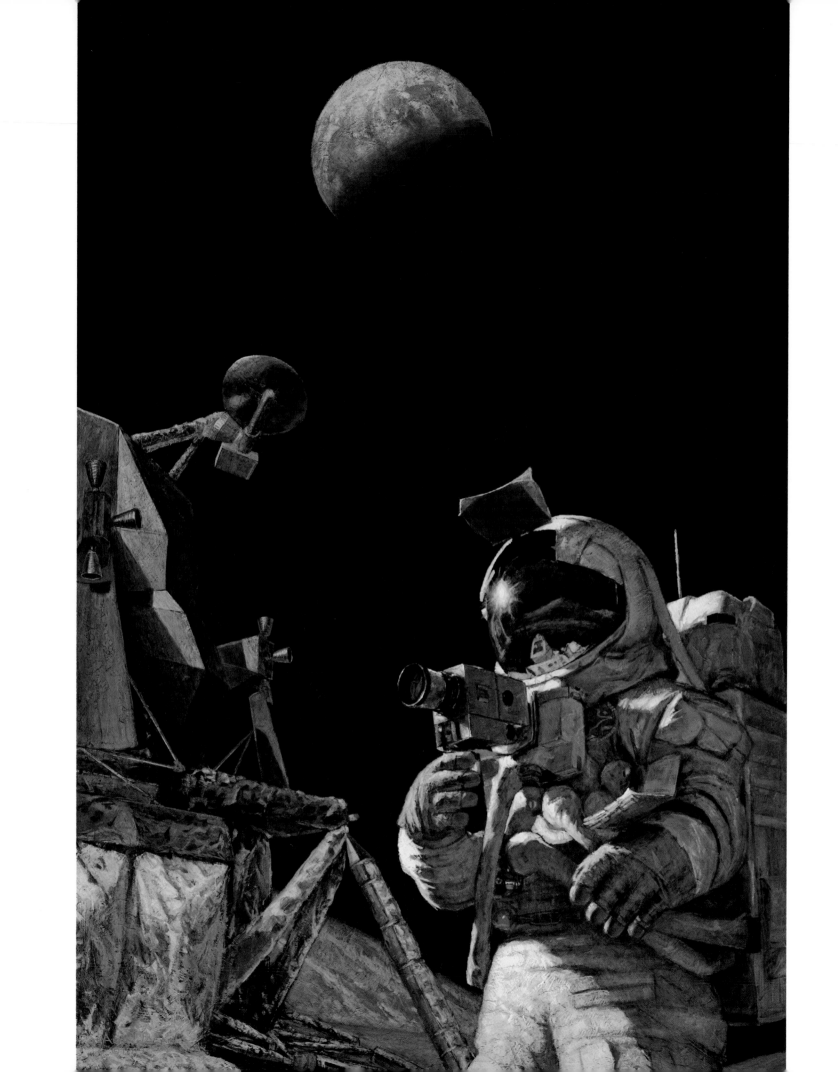

EPILOGUE
THE ENDLESS FRONTIER

WHEN GENE CERNAN, Ron Evans, and Jack Schmitt left the moon in December 1972, no one—especially not the astronauts—could have imagined they would be the last humans in the twentieth century to travel there.

Going to the moon took more than rocket power. It took more than the most advanced technology. It took money—*a lot* of money. Most important, the American people and their leaders had to want to go. But after the United States won the moon race with Apollo 11's landing, the general public was less interested, and space no longer seemed to be an important part of the cold war. Soon NASA had a new goal: to lower the cost of getting into Earth orbit with a reusable Space Shuttle. After December 1972, Americans stopped going to the moon. No one else has been there since then.

Looking back, it seems incredible how quickly Apollo began, and how quickly it ended. Just four years after Frank Borman's Apollo 8 crew made the first lunar voyage, Apollo 17's Gene Cernan and Jack Schmitt took the final moonwalk. Cernan has said it is as if President Kennedy "reached far into the twenty-first century, grabbed a decade of time and slipped it neatly into the 1960's."

Today, NASA is again planning for lunar missions, and its astronaut corps—which now includes both women and men—is working to help create new lunar vehicles, equipment, and techniques. No one can be sure when we will be moonbound again. But the voyages of Apollo have shown that it can be done—if we *choose* to go.

Only a few years before John Kennedy challenged the nation to put a man on the moon, most people thought of a lunar voyage as pure science fiction. And yet, once the challenge was accepted, it took only *eight years* for it to be met. Apollo—one of the greatest group achievements in history—is proof that when humans really work together they can accomplish seemingly impossible things.

COSMIC JOURNEY (1989): To go on a cosmic journey, one must leave the planet Earth far behind, an idea more than a little frightening. But on the journey, one will be treated to an incomparable sight: the Earth in its totality. It isn't possible to recognize the continents from the moon, because cloud patterns cover much of the Earth at any given time. The only change to the delicate blue-and-white pattern is an occasional small yellow-orange shape: a desert . . . but which one? It is almost impossible to tell. Here Jack Schmitt is taking a few photographs on a short cosmic journey. He is an astronaut—part explorer, part scientist and, however briefly, a wide-eyed tourist.

And Apollo has taught us something else, something precious: exploration offers us a new view of ourselves and our universe. Seeing the Earth from the moon has shown us that ours is a tiny and fragile planet, a world to be cherished and protected.

Whoever follows in the Apollo astronauts' lunar footsteps will have many exciting stories to tell when they come home. They will talk about the joy of bouncing in the moon's one-sixth gravity. They will share what it was like to stand on a bright and ancient wilderness, unchanged for billions of years, under a brilliant sun. And they will try to describe how they felt looking up into the blackness at the Earth, distant and beautiful.

The moon is only the first stop on an endless journey of exploration. Someday, humans will explore the planet Mars, 35 million miles away; Earth will be no more than a bright, bluish star in the night sky. Even then, they will have barely left home. Beyond our solar system lie other stars, other solar systems, other discoveries. Someday, humans will make those voyages. And when they do, they will look back on Apollo as humanity's first step toward the stars.

AN ASTRONAUT'S JOURNEY (2003): *Seasoned military test pilots were NASA's first choice for astronauts; flying high-performance airplanes provided the fundamental building blocks needed to fly a spaceship. However, moonwalkers need to select and collect rocks and dirt samples, deploy experiments, and make technical observations. So NASA gave us pilots extensive training as geologists—classroom lectures, laboratory study, and field trips to the sites that our instructors thought would most nearly represent what we might find on the moon. Because of this, a very vocal segment of the scientific community wanted to send a bona fide geologist/pilot, not a pilot/geologist like the rest of us. Jack Schmitt, shown here, was a talented geologist who was sent for flight training with the air force after being selected as an astronaut rather than the other way around. And Jack flew a great mission.*

ABOUT THE PAINTINGS

WHEN I FIRST STARTED to paint my story and the stories of my fellow Apollo astronauts, I came up against a unique problem. I had lived inside the adventure that was Apollo. I flew the spacecraft, wore the suit, and walked on another world—but I couldn't go back there.

Without being able to go back to the moon, how could I make paintings that were accurate and beautiful, and allowed people to connect with our Apollo experiences?

At first, I studied the NASA photographs from the moon, looking for images that would help relate the stories I wanted to tell. At the same time, I took countless photographs of everything from museum exhibits featuring space vehicles and hardware to NASA suit technicians posing in space suits, and used them as resource material. I began honing the technique of painting white subjects under intense lighting conditions, in a gray landscape, with a black sky. Each painting I finished brought me closer to where I wanted to be.

Finally, I realized that I needed to use small models of astronauts, LMs, lunar rovers, and other space hardware. (I built them to scale with the astronaut models about 12 inches high, and the LM about 32 inches high.) It was the only way I could accurately duplicate what we astronaut-explorers did on the moon.

Over the years, I've also refined the surface upon which I paint. I begin by cutting to size a sheet of a special plywood used to manufacture wooden airplanes—real ones, not models. I cover that plywood with a thick acrylic modeling paste. Then I press into it replicas of my lunar boots, as if I am walking across the painting, and make "footprints" just like the ones that we Apollo astronauts left in the lunar dust.

Since the moon is a rugged place, I wanted to add that kind of texture to my art. I use a heavy metal geology hammer—the same one I used on the moon to drive in the staff that held up our American flag and to pound in the core tube to obtain soil samples. With the hammer, I dig into the surface, pound at it, and scrape it. Next comes a sharp-edged bit that was on the cutting edge of one of the core tubes. Now I use it to make round indentations on the surface of the paintings.

There are also three physical things that I add to my paintings.

Several years ago, a friend of mine who is the director of a museum with an extensive collection of space hardware received our Apollo 12 spacecraft for display. When he opened the shipping container, he found that tiny portions of the charred heat shield that had protected us during the fiery re-entry at 25,000 miles per hour had shaken loose in transit. He collected this heat-shield material and sent it to me.

He also collected and sent pieces of foil insulation from the command module tunnel hatch.

I really wanted to have a small chip of lunar rock to grind up, so that I could put a little bit into each painting. Contrary to what some people think, NASA did not give any of us astronauts a moon rock as a souvenir. What they did give us were the American flags, NASA emblems, and Apollo mission patches we wore on our space suits. For years, mine were neatly framed and hanging on the wall of my study. One day I looked at them and realized that they were dirty with moon dust. I cut off a portion of these emblems and chopped them into small bits.

I place each of these things on the surface of the art in progress and paint over them as I continue working.

And so, within my paintings now are small bits of the charred heat shield and pieces of foil from the spaceship I flew to the moon, and minute amounts of moon dust that coated my space suit as I walked and worked on the Ocean of Storms.

—ALAN BEAN

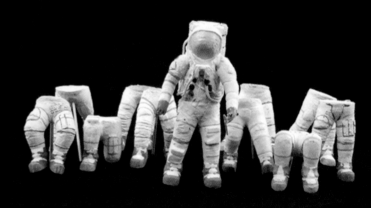
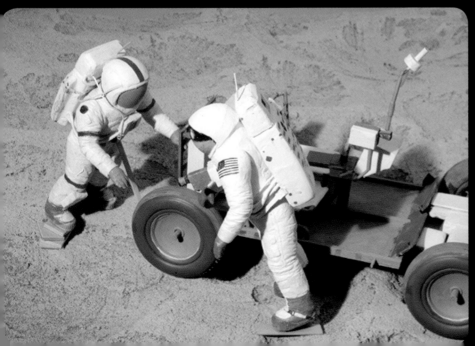

THE WRITE STUFF:
HOW WE WROTE THIS BOOK

ANDREW SAYS: I was born in 1956, the year before the space age began, and as I grew up, the space program grew up with me. As a small child, I fell in love with astronomy—especially the moon and the planets. I read everything I could get my hands on about what it might be like to visit other worlds. By the time I was in grade school, I knew that within a few years people would actually be going to the moon. I could hardly wait.

I was in junior high school when the Apollo missions began, and I camped out in front of the TV for every one of them, with models of the spacecraft and maps of the moon. During a trip to the Kennedy Space Center with my parents in April 1969, a couple of months before my thirteenth birthday, I even met several Apollo astronauts. Through an amazing bit of luck, we had chosen to stay at the same motel where the astronauts stayed when they were in town.

And the very first astronaut I met, believe it or not, was Alan Bean, who was training for his Apollo 12 mission. (The picture my dad took of Alan and

me that day is on the back flap of this book.) Even then, Alan was interested in art, and when I showed him my own drawing of an astronaut walking on the moon, he gave me a few pointers on how to make it better.

Seven months later, I was glued to the TV when Alan and his crewmates, Pete Conrad and Dick Gordon, went to the moon. All of the moonwalkers were "ultimate heroes" to me—but here was one I had actually met.

Of course, my greatest dream was that someday I would follow in the lunar footsteps of Bean and the rest of the Apollo moonwalkers. After I graduated from high school, I went to Brown University to study planetary geology, planning to someday apply to NASA to be a scientist-astronaut. In the summer of 1976 I was even able to take part in the first Mars landing, Viking 1.

Not long after that, I realized I would never be an astronaut, because of my medical history. So what did I want to do with my life? I found the answer a

Andrew Chaikin and Victoria Kohl in the lunar modular simulator at the Cradle of Aviation Museum, Garden City, NY.

couple of years after I graduated from Brown, when I switched from actually doing science to writing about it. Books had always been my "passport" to space, and it wasn't long before I decided I wanted to write one myself.

In 1985 I began working on a book about the Apollo astronauts. I was determined to tell the story of each lunar mission through the eyes of the astronauts themselves. I spent hours talking to all but one of the twenty-four lunar astronauts—Apollo 13's Jack Swigert had died in 1982.

In another great coincidence, the first astronauts I interviewed for the book were Alan Bean and his Apollo 12 crewmates, and I kept going from there. I also talked to many others who worked on Apollo, from flight directors to geologists. I read thousands of pages of mission communications transcripts and the astronauts' post-flight debriefings. I watched video of the TV transmissions from every flight. And I read countless books and interviews the astronauts had done since Apollo.

It took me eight years to finish my book, *A Man* on the Moon: The Voyages of the Apollo Astronauts, which was published in 1994. A few years after it came out, actor Tom Hanks—who had read my book while he was making the movie *Apollo 13*—used *A Man on the Moon* as the basis for his twelve-part HBO miniseries *From the Earth to the Moon.* I was a consultant on the production, and even had a tiny acting role in the first episode, as the host of *Meet the Press.*

I feel incredibly lucky to have grown up when humans were first leaving our planet and exploring another world, and I want other people to feel that excitement. Writing *Mission Control, This Is Apollo,* I've relied on the assistance of my wife, Vicki, who is a writer and editor with a long-standing love of space exploration. You can find out more about me, my other books, and my school visits at my Web site, www.andrewchaikin.com.

VICTORIA SAYS: I was always fascinated by space exploration, saving all space-related issues of *National Geographic* and *Life* magazines, and even collecting moon jewelry and Christmas ornaments. But my serious reading about the moon landings began when I discovered Andy's book, *A Man on the Moon.* After that I read everything I could find in new and used bookstores and libraries about the Apollo program and space history—from the development of the rocket planes to the engineers designing the spacecraft to lunar geology. When Andy and I met in 2000, he noticed that my bookshelves looked just like his! We got married in 2001, and have since begun writing books together.

ON RESEARCH AND SOURCES

My research for *Mission Control, This Is Apollo* actually began more than twenty years ago when I was working on the book that would become *A Man on the Moon*. That book has detailed notes; here, I have listed some of the most important primary sources, and a few others that are also great for your own "space exploration."

PEOPLE INTERVIEWED

APOLLO ASTRONAUTS: Edwin E. "Buzz" Aldrin Jr., William A. Anders, Neil A. Armstrong, Alan L. Bean, Frank Borman, Eugene A. Cernan, Michael Collins, Charles "Pete" Conrad Jr., R. Walter Cunningham, Charles M. Duke Jr., Ronald E. Evans, Richard F. Gordon Jr., Fred W. Haise Jr., James B. Irwin, James A. Lovell Jr., T. Kenneth Mattingly II, James A. McDivitt, Edgar D. Mitchell, Stuart A. Roosa, Walter M. Schirra Jr., Harrison H. "Jack" Schmitt, Russell L. "Rusty" Schweickart, David R. Scott, Alan B. Shepard Jr., Donald K. Slayton, Thomas P. Stafford, Alfred M. Worden, John W. Young

FLIGHT DIRECTORS AND CONTROLLERS: John Aaron, Steven Bales, Christopher C. Kraft, Eugene F. Kranz, Glynn Lunney

OTHER INTERVIEWEES

The dozens of people I interviewed included Apollo's geologists, program managers, historians, and mission planners, and NASA administrators and managers, simulator instructors and supervisors, space craft engineers, and space suit technicians, as well as the wives and children of the astronauts.

FURTHER READING

Armstrong, Neil, Michael Collins, and Edwin E. Aldrin Jr. *First on the Moon.* Boston: Little, Brown and Company, 1970.

Brooks, Courtney G., James M. Grimwood, and Loyd S. Swenson Jr. *Chariots for Apollo: A History of Manned Lunar Spacecraft.* NASA SP-4205. Washington, D.C.: Government Printing Office, 1979. (Available online at http://history.nasa.gov/SP-4205/cover.html)

Collins, Michael. *Carrying the Fire: An Astronaut's Journeys.* New York: Farrar, Straus, and Giroux, 1974.

Cortright, Edgar M., ed. *Apollo Expeditions to the Moon.* NASA SP-350. Washington, D.C.: Government Printing Office, 1975. (Available online at http://history.nasa.gov/SP-350/cover.html)

Hacker, Barton C., and James M. Grimwood. *On the Shoulders of Titans: A History of Project Gemini.* NASA History Series. Washington. D.C.: NASA, 1977. (Available online at http://history.nasa.gov/SP-4203/toc.htm)

Murray, Charles, and Catherine Bly Cox. *Apollo: The Race to the Moon.* New York: Simon and Schuster, 1989.

Thimmesh, Catherine. *Team Moon: How 400,000 People Landed Apollo 11 on the Moon.* Boston: Houghton Mifflin Company, 2006.

Wilhelms, Don E. *To a Rocky Moon: A Geologist's History of Lunar Exploration.* Tucson: The University of Arizona Press, 1993.

WEB SITES

Apollo 11 30th Anniversary. NASA's Apollo history Web site: http://history.nasa.gov/ap11ann/introduction. htm

Apollo Lunar Surface Journal. Features interviews with many of the moonwalkers and extensive audio and video clips of the missions: http://history.nasa. gov/alsj/frame.html

Hubble Site. Hubble Space Telescope images and information about the universe: http://hubblesite.org/

NASA: Lunar and Planetary Science. More advanced information from NASA on lunar science: http://nssdc. gsfc.nasa.gov/planetary/planets/moonpage.html

NASA Jet Propulsion Laboratory: Photojournal. Spacecraft images of the solar system, including planets, moons, asteroids, and comets: http://photojournal. jpl.nasa.gov/index.html

Project Apollo Archive: The Apollo Image Gallery: www. apolloarchive.com/apollo_gallery.html

Smithsonian National Air and Space Museum: www.nasm. si.edu

Space.com. News about space: www.space.com

World Book at NASA: Moon: www.nasa.gov/worldbook/ moon_worldbook.html

OTHER MEDIA

Apogee Books: (www.cgpublishing.com) has published a series of mission overviews containing transcripts of debriefing sessions and CD-ROMs of historic film footage, photographs, and recent interviews.

Spacecraft Films: (www.spacecraftfilms.com) offers DVD sets of every Apollo mission, featuring in-flight television transmissions including every moonwalk, as well as rare film documentation of preflight activities and launches. Other sets chronicle Mercury, Gemini, the Saturn V, and other spaceflight-related subjects.

Documentaries: There have been a number of documentaries covering the Apollo program, the most recent of which (as of this writing) are *The Wonder of It All,* featuring interviews with Apollo moonwalkers, and the Discovery Channel's multi-part documentary *The NASA Missions: When We Left Earth.*

ACKNOWLEDGMENTS

This book would not have been written without Sharyn November, our editor at Viking Children's Books, who conceived of the project and whose singular commitment made it happen. We *do* feel a bit responsible for her transformation into an obsessed space geek, however.

We celebrate our readers, and we hope this book inspires in them a love of exploration.

Janet Pascal, our copyeditor, had a keen eye and many helpful suggestions.

Special thanks go to the astronauts who shared stories of their lunar experiences and gave all of us a taste of what it's like to visit another world.

Extra special thanks to Alan Bean, for his insights, his friendship, and, of course, his wonderful paintings.   —Andrew Chaikin and Victoria Kohl

Jim Hoover has done outstanding design work—it's lively, colorful, and there's something interesting to look at on every page. He is as much of a part of this book as Andy, Vicki, and I.   —Alan Bean

INDEX

Note: Page numbers in *italics* indicate paintings